Dear

The resurgence of China is the most important political and economic event of our times. Her modernisation and urbanisation provide the directional signals for the shift of global power to the East.

This book of lectures, given on RTÉ Radio by a group of experienced Sinophiles (two of whom are from Treasury Holdings), provides a snapshot of the current position and the social and historical context into which it fits.

For Treasury Holdings, China represents our most important non-European location and the future seat of one-third of our global activities. We hope the book assists your understanding of the enormous part China will come to play in all our lives.

Richard Barrett
Chief Executive Officer
Treasury Holdings Group

 TREASURY HOLDINGS

about, we Irish have been once again impressed with how tightly we are bound together as nation to nation in this world. The laws of economics do not respect national boundaries; collapse in one economy can mean devastation in another. As a small, open economy, we Irish are learning the hard lesson of what that entails. It is a lesson worth learning, if it means that we can begin to understand that the Ireland of coming times must evolve within the context of a new community, one in which China is now taking its place as one of our most valued partners.

But why has it taken so long? There are two answers: one is that Ireland has been, since its founding as a sovereign republic, fairly self-preoccupied. The other answer is simply that, up to now, most Irish people have encountered China only as little islands of isolated experience. They may have visited the gardens at Birr Castle, for instance, perhaps only then learning how many of its trees and exquisite flowers came from China. They may have wondered at the jade books or elaborately embroidered imperial Dragon Robes at Dublin's Chester Beatty Library, but without knowing what connections the Qianlong Emperor had with Ireland. Or, nearer to home, they might have met some of the more than 11,000 Chinese nationals who now live in Ireland. But what relation can one discover between these different experiences? How can one actually connect them up?

Until recently, it was relatively difficult to create any sustained interest in a country apparently so distant. And today, despite its rising importance, we in Ireland still have a great deal to learn about China. Certainly the sheer disparity between the two countries makes initial comparisons appear a little absurd. In terms of population alone, China's 1.34 billion means that, effectively, one of five people on this earth is Chinese. By way of contrast, the island of Ireland's six million people could fit comfortably within a small Chinese city. Yet in world terms, Ireland and China are, in some surprising ways, comparable. Both China and Ireland have evolved through long, and often turbulent, histories. Both have a valued ancient heritage which they are striving to incorporate into present-day practice. And both have moved, in a matter of generations, from a traditional culture to a

.1.

Ireland through a Chinese Mirror

✲

JERUSHA McCORMACK

For years now, looking at China from Ireland often seemed like looking at a country through the wrong end of a telescope. Not only did China seem very strange, it also appeared to be very far away. Within a little more than a year, all of that has changed. One might date the shift of perspective from 12 May 2008, when a great earthquake devastated the area around Chengdu, a city in southwest China, sweeping away as many as 70,000 people. With it was swept away, perhaps forever, the sense that China was a distant place. No strangers to tragedy ourselves, the hearts of the Irish people have gone out to the people of China: to those that have lost their homes, their relatives and, in partic- ular, their only child.

Now, in 2009, that sense of immediacy has been again brought home by another crisis: the sudden and shocking collapse of the global economy. In trying to understand how this has come

UACHTARÁN NA hÉIREANN
PRESIDENT OF IRELAND

MESSAGE FROM PRESIDENT McALEESE

Ireland and China enjoy a long and intriguing relationship, even if much of it has remained hidden for too long from wider view. What is most surprising is not that we share such a long history together, but rather the great diversity of that relationship: ranging from diplomatic missions and deepening business links to musical traditions, from literary affinities to botanical excursions, as this publication and the related RTE Thomas Davis Lectures Series recount. China and Ireland have both had complex and turbulent histories, both countries have ancient heritages that are deeply valued, and both have experienced in recent decades a process of transformation from a traditional way of life to one characterised by dramatic economic progress and prosperity and much greater global engagement.

This year China and Ireland celebrate 30 years of diplomatic relations and so there is a particular timeliness also about this initiative and its review of the long intertwining of relationships between our two countries. Both countries have come a long way in the intervening three decades and we have made at least some of this journey together. Irish businesses have thrived in China's vibrant economy and Irish consumers have greatly benefited from the staggering output of China's manufacturing sector. Ireland has in turn been host to many thousands of young, educated and hardworking Chinese people who have helped build and share in Ireland's own dramatic growth, particularly in the last decade.

As President, I was privileged to make a State Visit to China in 2003, having previously been there as Pro-Vice Chancellor of the Queens University of Belfast in 1997. During that fascinating State Visit I said that we looked forward to exploring the opportunities not just for prosperity but friendship and mutual cultural curiosity. Recent events have shown how deeply interdependent the world has become. Looking to the future it will be vital to widen and strengthen the connections and interrelationships that we share as a global community, including with China. That is why initiatives such as this publication and the related Thomas Davis Lectures Series by RTE are so important and I look forward to seeing more links and connections of this kind as the relationship between Ireland and China continues to grow and develop.

Mary McAleese

MARY McALEESE
PRESIDENT OF IRELAND

16 JANUARY, 2009

Contents

✩

CHINA AND THE IRISH
First published 2009
by New Island
2 Brookside
Dundrum Road
Dublin 14

www.newisland.ie

ISBN 978-1-84840-042-9

British Library Cataloguing Data. A CIP catalogue record for this book is available from the British Library.

Printed in Spain by Castuera Industrias Graficas

10 9 8 7 6 5 4 3 2 1

China *and the* Irish

THE THOMAS DAVIS LECTURE SERIES 2008

Edited by Jerusha McCormack

RTÉ NEW ISLAND

modern (perhaps even a post-modern) one. And finally, both suffer from the complications of a newly rich society now seeking its own definition of what it means to be Chinese – or Irish.

China is a very old nation; but a century of turmoil has forced it to seek new versions of itself and its culture. Likewise, we Irish are actively engaged in reinventing who we are. Until recently many were reluctant to think of the North as 'Irish'. But now the inclusion of the North in a larger conception of Ireland encourages this series to bring in such a personage as Lord Macartney: born and bred in County Antrim – and a graduate of Trinity College, Dublin. The first essay here examines his role as head of the first British Embassy to the Qianlong Emperor of China in 1793. Another Antrim man was Robert Hart (1835–1911), who served as Inspector-General of China's Maritime Customs Service during the last decades of the nineteenth century. Hart was exceptional in that he was trusted equally by both his British and his Chinese masters. During his lengthy career, Hart imported some of the best of his own culture to China: in particular, his love of music. It seems that, in all respects, Hart was the model of a gentleman, in both civilisations: admired by Westerners for his deft diplomacy in complex international affairs and by the Chinese for his incorruptible, upright and mannerly presence.

It is thus significant that Robert Hart thought of himself not merely as British but also as Irish. More than that, as Richard O'Leary's essay argues, it was this very sense of Irishness which made it possible for Hart to be so effective an administrator in China. Being Irish, even today, is a complex fate. It was more so at a time when Ireland was beginning to assert its independence from Britain. If Hart identified himself as an Irishman, he also, depending on occasion, called himself English, British and an Ulsterman.

Although this example does not fit with any simple version of Irishness, it is exactly this sense of multiple – and, possibly at times, competing – senses of identity which is characteristic of being Irish. At this crucial moment in our national history, we have a president who was, like Robert Hart, originally from the

China *and the* Irish

North of Ireland, a graduate of Queen's University and both a British and an Irish citizen. And perhaps it is exactly this richly complex sense of identity that will now enable Ireland to enter the new century as a capable and effective member of the emerging world order.

That we have already begun to redefine our Irish identity as multiple and open is clear. Twenty years ago, many would not have accepted such a figure as Oscar Wilde as 'one of us' precisely because of a very restricted view of who was Irish and who was not. For among academic circles, at least, Wilde's own sense of his origins, as well as our sense of what he made of them, had proved problematic. But now we not only we claim Wilde as Irish but even go on to ask what part Wilde's Irishness played in his startling appropriation of Zhuangzi (Chuang Tsu in the old-fashioned Wade-Giles romanisation), a radical Chinese thinker of the fourth century BC.

Yet vestiges of those old restrictions on what can and cannot be deemed as 'Irish' still remain. For instance, how many in Ireland today accept our hereditary aristocrats as being as authentically Irish as someone, say, from the Gaeltacht? Are they merely a relic of our colonial past that we would prefer to ignore? Or are we ready to appropriate as part of our national heritage the magnificent gardens in Birr Castle demesne? These gardens are the result of three generations of the Parsons family – otherwise known as the Earls of Rosse, who stem from one of the oldest Anglo-Irish families in Ireland – identifying and importing into Ireland some of China's most exquisite plants. That history, largely unknown, is recounted here in print for the first time by the Seventh Earl of Rosse, Brendan Parsons.

Or again, what does the history of Irish missionaries, both Catholic and Protestant, tell us about ourselves in what is said to be a 'post-Catholic' Ireland? Can we acknowledge that the same 'heroism and zeal' which led these missionaries to prepare for self-sacrifice in China also fuelled the 1916 Easter Rising – and its cult of heroic martyrdom? Is their vision of the missionary movement as reviving a glorious past still part of our own vision of Ireland – as a country that may yet have a mission to the world, albeit now larger than that of spreading Christianity to the pagan world of early medieval Europe?

As these examples demonstrate, one way of connecting up these experiences is to seek to understand how relations with an *Other* – even a very alien *Other* – can become a new way of relating to ourselves. Accordingly, in this series of essays, China often offers a mirror to Ireland. Through its reflection, we will see how and why the Chieftains could go to Beijing in 1983 and, without prior practice, hold a jam session with Chinese traditional musicians. In the process, Hwee-San Tan will reveal as much about traditional music practice in Ireland as in China.

But, as in a true mirror, the picture is not always flattering. As Fintan O'Toole shows, Irish workers' hostility to Chinese workers in mid-nineteenth-century America culminated in the Chinese Exclusion Act of 1882. Instigated by a popular movement, this act – for the first and only time in American history – succeeded in banning immigrants from one specific country of origin.

What does this history imply, if anything, about the kind of welcome a new set of Chinese immigrants might face in Ireland today? How do current reports that most Chinese student-workers claim to have experienced some form of racial discrimination square with our own perception of ourselves? As Ruadhán Mac Cormaic observes in his essay, the Chinese immigrant community here is among the most fragmented and possibly the most stressed of all our new arrivals. Are we courageous enough to meditate on this mirror-image replay of our own history – this time on our own home ground?

As reflected in the mirror of China, Ireland appears as a relatively new nation still seeking to define its role in the world. We are known as a small, politically neutral country. For many, our fight for independence from Great Britain has symbolically absolved us from its imperial past. Like the People's Republic of China, we also call ourselves a republic. The fact that both nations lay claim to this definition of themselves should give us some pause. The ideals of *our* republic are derived from the ideas that inspired American independence and then the French revolution. The big words which have enabled our own definition of nation – liberty, equality, democracy – resonate everywhere in our public debates and our private expectations.

But in China these big words traditionally have had little resonance. The Chinese word for 'democracy', for instance, was introduced from Japan only a century ago. Today in China an understanding of this concept is only just emerging, not necessarily in our sense, but in terms of encouraging greater accountability throughout the governmental system: that of the central government to the people and the accountability of those appointed to represent the people to the central government. But even as it gains in cultural resonance, 'democracy' cannot operate there as it does in the West in the absence of another Western concept – 'equality'. China is a top-down place: authority rests in a central government at the top of an intensely hierarchical society – and such has been the case for more than 2,000 years. There is no relation in China which is between equals, except arguably that between friends. All else fits into a hierarchical scale which is accepted as if ordained since time immemorial, whether within the family or its cognate structures in governance.

In what sense, then, is China a 'republic'? In the sense that the Chinese government asserts that it embodies the will of the collectivity and therefore strives (in the words of Mao Zedong) to 'serve the people'. But given the difference in the way these two worlds are governed, and the principles by which they are organised, it should come as no surprise that they also differ as to the nature of human beings and the multiple rights that modern Western thinking attributes to individuals. All members of the United Nations – China, as well as Ireland and the United States – are deemed to be supporters of the 1948 UN Universal Declaration of Human Rights (which recently celebrated its sixtieth anniversary). However few, if any, of the citizens of UN countries actually read what is written in this document or learn from the history of how it came to be formulated.

For those who take the trouble to examine it, it is clear that the document falls into two distinct parts. The first part, comprising the initial twenty or so articles, was composed under the influence of Enlightenment principles which depend heavily on such ideas as Equality and Freedom as now central in modern Western thinking about Democracy. These would include the right to equality before the law as well as to freedom of expression, of movement and of assembly, among others. The last nine articles of the UN Declaration, on the other hand, comprise such social, economic and cultural rights as the right to food, housing, education, work and social protection. Consequently, in public debates about 'Human Rights', Western diplomats routinely assume that they are speaking to the first twenty articles, whereas those from China focus on the government's commitment to fulfilling the last nine. Thus while both protest that their own nations are indeed supporting human rights while the other side is violating them, each is implicitly referring to a different set of defining articles. The result is a dialogue of the deaf.

The way such delegates talk past each other is perhaps not always deliberate but more a matter of acculturation. To the Chinese, the 'human rights' which guarantee a people food, housing, education and jobs are *the* fundamental values. Indeed, over the past six decades, the Chinese government has made amazing strides in feeding, housing, educating and employing a massive and largely poor population. In relation to Tibet, the Chinese government points to the rapid modernisation of what they consider an underdeveloped economy or to the special treatment accorded to minorities in China in regard to university entrance or their absolution from the One-Child Policy which holds for the majority Han population.

From this perspective, it might be said that the West has been slow to give credit to the Chinese government for the giant strides they have made in feeding, housing and otherwise caring for their huge population. For in the West, social, economic and cultural rights are regarded by many not as rights but as 'hopes' or 'aspirations'. This is the stance of the US Senate, which has consistently refused to ratify the UN International Covenant on Social, Economic and Cultural Rights (as all other developed countries, including Ireland, have done). Former US Ambassador to the UN Jeanne Kirkpatrick was quite explicit on their status when she referred to social, economic and cultural rights as a 'letter to Santa Claus'; while her successor described the International Covenant as 'little more than an empty vessel into which vague hopes and inchoate expectations can be poured'.

Contrast this ideological orientation, widely shared by American elites, with one of Confucius's simpler but profound statements: 'It is a disgrace to be well fed while the people are hungry' (*Analects* 8.13). Indeed, given the emerging global food crisis, a renewed emphasis on the last nine articles of the Universal Declaration of Human Rights may now be imperative for all people of good will.

Above all, what this disparity of views illustrates is the way America tends to position itself as an extreme of Western views. If America represents one extreme on these issues and China another, then where does Ireland fit in?

Historically, Ireland should, at least in theory, be as sympathetic to the last nine articles of the UN Declaration of Human Rights as to the first twenty. During much of its colonial past, the majority of Irish people was not housed nor educated nor even fed by the British government. In fact one of the Irish experiences to which Chinese students respond most sympathetically is the Great Famine; for they themselves experienced a devastating famine which killed an estimated 20 to 40 million people between the years 1958–61. But when the Chinese learn more about the politics of the Irish famine, and particularly about the lack of response from the British government, they are mystified.

This is because, I believe, the Chinese have little sense of another big Western word, 'ethnicity'. For a long time, the whole case for Irish nationhood – and British prejudice towards the Irish – rested on the conception of a distinctive Celtic 'race', as Irish ethnicity was then defined. Yet our insistence on our own difference baffles the Chinese. After all, as they are quick to point out, the Irish and the English *look* very much alike. But of course we now understand the case for Irish identity resides not on an assertion of a difference in race but of *ethos*: the sense that the Irish 'feel different' from the British. And in fact the Irish *are* different. To point to this difference, an Irish person may cite a distinctive language, customary traditions – and religion (which had been, in fact, the 'old religion' of England). Some would even argue that the Irish have a different – and distinctive – mentality and way of thinking.

Such a difference is invisible in the Chinese world because 'ethnicity' – as a name for a distinct ethos or mentality – is not recognised there. Thus the 55 or so minority cultures that inhabit the People's Republic of China are referred to as 'nationalities' – not as distinct ethnic groups. A 'nationality' is an official construct – a geopolitical one imposed by bureaucratic authority. In calling Tibetans, for instance, members of a 'nationality', the Chinese authorities are not allowing for difference of language or religion but only for definition by official boundaries – moreover ones that have been redrawn quite arbitrarily over the years.

Two issues thus cloud understanding of the current situation in Tibet: a systematic narrowness in defining 'human rights' and a blindness towards ethnic difference. Resolution of these crucial issues requires education on each side – and patient diplomacy. But that crucial diplomatic work, recently restarted in the form of talks with the representatives of the Dalai Lama, often seems impeded by a newly assertive Chinese nationalism. By many Chinese this nationalism is welcomed as a way of unifying a country battered by a century of revolutions, the last of which – the 1978 introduction of 'capitalism with Chinese character-istics' – has overturned much of the old Maoist rhetoric. Today the fading ideology of Communism is being replaced by promoting the 'new China'. But what is this 'new China'? The answer is only gradually emerging.

Over here, this question echoes a popular 1970s parlour game asking 'Where is the real Ireland?' As we know, the answers would typically be divided between East and West, Dublin and Connemara. In those days, no one would have named the North. And yet, by the tortuous path which has led to a redefinition of 'the real Ireland', we have now come to include both North and South as well as East and West.

But even as we have come to this accommodation, Ireland is once again changing as, over the last decades, it has become home to people from 150 different countries, speaking almost 170 languages. Of this international community, a sizeable group is now from China. Many of these will return to China, but others will stay. And they will become part of a new generation – not only an Irish but now a global generation, making their lives, as they will forge their identities, between and across whole cultures and civilisations. What then will it mean to be 'Irish'? And where will they locate, if anywhere, 'the real Ireland'?

Just as we are now beginning to accept that there are many Irelands, each as 'real' as the other, one does not have to travel far to discover there is not one but many Chinas. The north and south of China are as different from each other as the far west is from the east coast. Those 55 separate 'nationalities' recognised by the Chinese government speak a total of 236 different languages. These exist in a nation defined largely by the Han Chinese, who claim to make up 92 per cent of the population. The official policy is that minority groups should evolve in parallel to the dominant culture. The fact that recent developments are now encouraging the majority Han population to settle in Tibet means that Tibetans feel their own distinctive culture and traditions are being undermined by the majority culture. As Irish people, we know from our own history, and in particular from that of the North, the consequences of such developments. And we can now say to China that, among these islands, it has taken about 700 years to begin to resolve the ensuing difficulties.

These are the kinds of reflections – and cultural parallels – that prompted the suggestion that China could benefit from an Irish Studies Programme. The Beijing Foreign Studies University, where I have been Visiting Professor, is a small elite university where the Chinese government traditionally trains its personnel for the Foreign Ministry. They already boast a prestigious American Studies Programme, as well as British, Australian and Canadian Studies centres. But in all of China there was, as yet, no other official Irish Studies Programme. When informed of the proposal, the Dean of the School of English and International Studies, Professor Sun Youzhong, was enthusiastic. His response was only matched in force by that of the current Irish Ambassador to China, Declan Kelleher, as backed by the Irish Department of Foreign

Affairs. Working with the support of the National University of Ireland, Maynooth, the Irish Studies Centre was opened in March 2007, only a year after it was proposed.

Teaching in this new centre has been quite an experience. Although some students know Ireland as the land of literary Nobel Prize winners – and of *Riverdance* (which created a sensation in China) – many believed it was still part of the United Kingdom. Mostly the Chinese public is simply shocked by its size. After being told that the entire population of the Irish Republic would fit into the (northeastern) city of Harbin, one Chinese professor held up her hands as if measuring a child. 'So small, so small,' she crooned. 'Couldn't have any large problems.'

We may be a small country, I assured her, but our problems are large – global in fact. And it is these problems, and our efforts to resolve them, that make us valuable to China. Whereas Ireland's recent economic success is admired by the Chinese, they need to know that we are already paying the price: whether it is in cities that cannot drink their water or the love-affair with the automobile which has blighted urban as well as rural landscapes. In the cities of the new China, water resources and the effects of rampant car-culture are already becoming almost intractable issues. Among these essays, Pauline Byrne, an Irish city planner who has worked in China, meditates on the development of the new mega-cities in China. Here again the outcomes of overdevelopment in Ireland or of commercial pressures which are emptying our inner cities of residents or even the overdependence on the construction industry as a driver of economic growth might prove instructive, if only as small moral tales on the perils of precipitate urban development.

From another perspective, Ireland might offer China some positive precedents. In terms of the environment, we have already provided China with a model they followed recently by taxing the use of plastic bags. The Chinese have even proposed to implement a universal smoking ban, though its enforcement has been delayed due to popular protest. Yet if Ireland's example were followed, the health status of the ordinary Chinese, already choking in some of the worst urban pollution in the world, would improve noticeably. Again, in terms of the market economy, China has adapted the most brutal, most unregulated form of laissez-faire capitalism. Although there have been some notable shifts of focus by the Chinese government in the last year or so, it still has a lot to learn from European countries, Ireland among them, about how they can now seek to mitigate the worst effects of the collapse of an unfettered market economy on the most vulnerable in society: the very young, the old, the sick, the rural, the unemployed.

More immediate to the Chinese students is the history of Ireland's invention of itself out of a colonial past and its struggle for independence. Accounts of Ireland's experience of famine – and foreign colonisation – are eagerly received by the Irish Studies students as vivid reminders of similar events within their own history. Starting in 1842 when the First Opium War gave Hong Kong to Britain, China suffered through a long series of what are still referred to as 'humiliating treaties'. These humiliations are still fresh in the minds of my Chinese students; so much so that, in teaching about Ireland, I have to be careful not to feed too obviously into the sense of victimhood that is traditionally a driving force behind both Irish – and now Chinese – nationalism. Not only is it too easy to do so, it is untrue to the actual complexities of the situation. In teaching Irish Studies, it is more fruitful, I have found, to try to describe Ireland's history under British rule for what in fact it was: a regime in which the Irish were both administrators as well as victims; slaveholders as well as indentured servants; nationalists as well as loyal servants of the British Empire. It is well to remind ourselves that Ireland has always had a complex fate which nationalist causes have often oversimplified for their own ends.

As is clear from these reflections, Ireland's new relationship with China will prove far more complex than merely one of exchange. While each has much to learn from the other, the two nations, so widely divergent in terms of scale, history and culture, may also act as mirrors, reflecting their own cultures from fresh and sometimes disconcerting angles. Although this might be a disorienting experience, attention must be paid; for China is now becoming a significant world power, one with which Ireland will need to deal every day. As entrepreneur Richard Barrett's essay illustrates, dealing with China entails going far beyond merely doing business: it must mean engaging with the culture itself. What else it may imply in terms of mutual enlightenment is yet to be explored. In this series of essays (originally written for the RTÉ Thomas Davis lectures), our speakers have been asked to look at specific links between Ireland and China as a way of opening up new ways of encountering China – but also as a way of arranging new encounters with ourselves.

.2.

 *Empires at Odds:*

The Qianlong Emperor
and Earl Macartney's British Mission

☆

SHANE MCCAUSLAND

The lectures in this year's Thomas Davis series explore 'new frontiers' between Ireland and China. But in fact, China has been known to Ireland for centuries. In 1298, Marco Polo dictated an account of his travels to Khubilai Khan's (r. 1260–94) court at Peking (Beijing); this was translated into Irish within a century – about a hundred and fifty years before its first translation into English.[1]

For the purposes of this lecture, though, 'history' begins with another pioneering mission to China just over two hundred years ago: the Macartney Mission.[2] It is a moment coloured and complicated by its geo-political context in the era of imperialism, of 'the British century' and the so-called 'Great Game' that was international diplomacy. In the late eighteenth century, Ireland was, of course, poised to become, through the Act of Union, part of the United Kingdom of Great Britain and Ireland under King George III (r. 1760–1820). China was under foreign – that is, Manchu – rule by the Qianlong emperor (r. 1736–95) of the Great Qing dynasty (1644–1911).

What should we today make of that first serious attempt at establishing diplomatic relations back in 1793? Who was this first ambassador to China, George, Earl Macartney? How did this Belfast-born, Trinity-educated diplomat come to receive this prestigious appointment? And how did he come to return to the Court of St James's bearing a singularly undiplomatic put-down, an edict from the Emperor of China addressed to King George?[3]

As an art historian of China, what interests me about this diplomatic episode is not its history – which has been mined for lessons both in China and the West – but the messages encoded in it as a piece of cultural theatre. Parts of the Chinese collection of the Chester Beatty Library in Dublin, such as imperial engravings, jade books and silk dragon robes, show how the Qianlong emperor used visual art and material culture to determine perceptions of him variously as a sage- or warrior-king by his subjects in China and foreign ambassadors alike. The visual record of diplomacy on both sides is also crucial. In addition to the Chester Beatty engravings on this topic are the drawings made by Macartney's staff of his audience and travels in China, which survive mostly in the British Library.

Let me first give some context to this mission. During the mid-eighteenth century, the vogue for China and things Chinese, known as *Chinoiserie*, swept across Europe. Tea from China was avidly drunk; architecture, painting, furniture design and fashion succumbed to the fever. Such an influential figure as Voltaire, intrigued by China, wrote a series of texts on its distinctive morals and values. In the business world, traders and merchants, particularly in Britain's East India Company, eyed China as one of the world's great untapped markets. Yet trading with China was increasingly restricted by the Qing government, which viewed with suspicion foreigners' attempts to expand trade. From 1760 on, in an attempt to control the numbers of foreign merchants, all trade was limited to one port far in the south of China at Canton (modern Guangzhou). Transactions were further hampered by laws requiring business to be conducted through the established middlemen, the *hong*s or trading houses. As the century wore on, the import of tea from China to the British Isles caused a growing trade imbalance. As a consequence, the East India Company increased pressure on the British government to engage in some form of trade diplomacy with China, to open up China to imports such as Bombay cotton and Bengal opium.

Then, at the high point of the Manchu Qing dynasty (1644–1911), eighteenth-century China felt no equal fascination with the West. For instance, the Jesuits, who had been bringing Christianity together with Western science and technology to China since the late sixteenth century, were quickly losing influence there as well as in Europe. Some branches of Western learning were still considered useful, such as for the regulation of the calendar. But in fine art, critics were largely unmoved by the European painting techniques of shading and perspective, which, from a traditional Chinese viewpoint, merely made subjects appear devoid of life.

It is curious, then, how the century witnessed a great partnership between an emperor of China and a court painter, although neither of them was actually Chinese. The Qing emperor, a Manchu, known as Qianlong (r. 1736–95), was conservative even for an absolute monarch. His sixty-year reign, and somewhat mawkish style of kingship, dominated the eighteenth century. His favourite court artist was the Italian Jesuit painter Giuseppe Castiglione (1688–1766), pioneer of a hybrid painting style which incorporated European techniques into Chinese media. Occasionally, Castiglione joined forces with Manchu and Chinese court painters to collaborate on more obviously Sino-European-styled paintings. With often breathtaking realism, Castiglione and his peers executed fine portraits of Qianlong in his many personae as emperor: as commander-in-chief seated in armour on his horse **[figure 1]**; graciously receiving tribute horses from Central Asian ambassadors; sitting in meditation as a Buddha; amusing himself at calligraphy in his studio; watching his courtiers out ice-skating at the New Year festival; and out hunting. In his later years at court, Castiglione was intimately involved in the portrayal of two sides of the Qianlong imperial persona: as the warrior-king expanding the territorial boundaries of China and as the patron of the arts with a fancy for intricate and complex architecture. The holdings of the Chester Beatty Library in Dublin provide insights into these activities.

Although it is not likely the Qianlong emperor wore any of the Qing dragon robes in the Chester Beatty collection, these imperial silk garments serve as tangible reminders of China's late imperial court ritual and social hierarchy. They are referred to generically as 'dragon robes' because of the imperial insignia of auspicious dragons embroidered all over them. Yellow silk was reserved exclusively for the emperor and empress's dragon robes, but robes in other colours bearing motifs of rank were used throughout the court to distinguish concubine from empress dowager and eunuch from grand secretary. Varied according to season and ritual or state occasion, court attire played a literal part in maintaining an absolutist system of government which upheld the emperor in his semi-divine position as the Son of Heaven.

To win Heaven's continued approval of his reign, and to assure himself of the status quo on earth, the emperor also undertook to bring glory on China by other means. One of the Qianlong emperor's acknowledged achievements as ruler was the consolidation of the area known as the 'western regions' under Qing rule. Through military interventions he quelled various long-running rebellions and 'pacified' these areas. This eighteenth-century form of empire-building also bolstered the emperor's legitimacy among his own Manchu people by showing him to be the epitome of a Manchu warrior-king.

One of the emperor's first campaigns was the 'pacification' of the Muslim peoples in what is now the far west of China, to the north of Tibet (1755–59). Castiglione was chief among those commanded to design a set of engravings commemorating the victories and showing the subjugated leaders being brought to Peking to pay tribute to the emperor. Such was its importance to him, the emperor had the set of designs sent to Paris to be engraved and printed (1766–74) by Charles-Nicholas Cochin (1715–90) and Jacques-Philippe Le Bas (1707–83), the royal engravers to the Bourbon court.[4]

The Chester Beatty Library has a set of these prints, known as *Quelling the Rebellion in the Western Regions*. One of the most successful designs by Castiglione is entitled 'The Relief of the Black River Camp' (*Heishui ying jiewei*), engraved by Le Bas in 1771. **[figure 2]** The scene is a battle sweeping across a vast, mountainous panorama. It shows the lifting of the siege on the camp at Qara usu (Black River), where Qing troops were encircled during the winter of 1758. In the engraving, the Qing forces led by mounted archers attack an overwhelmed enemy in headlong retreat to the right. In the central foreground on a promontory, the imposing Qing general Fude, attended by staff officers and mounted on a white pony, directs the fire of several cannon toward the enemy's flank. Nearby lie camels fitted with wooden crosses for carrying the artillery pieces. To the left, Qing engineers hastily rebuild a wooden bridge across the Black River as another regiment of cavalry patiently waits to cross. Behind them, standards and banners flutter over the liberated Qing encampment.

To the Chinese, this territorial expansion not only contributed to the greater glory of China but burnished the emperor's self-image as a Chinese sage-king. How did the Qianlong emperor impress upon his people the breadth of his learning? In the Chester Beatty collections are more than a dozen imperial jade books from this period. These are books literally engraved in stone. One of the boons of the territorial expansion in the western regions was that it enabled the Qianlong emperor, an inveterate collector of precious things, to obtain rich seams of China's most precious and revered substance: jade. Boulders were immediately shipped back to the capital where they were carved in the imperial workshops into thick sheets, before being engraved and gilded with the words of the emperor on all kinds of abstruse subjects –

as well as the emperor's own poems (or poems attributed to him). These books exemplify the emperor's much-professed love of learning, alongside his military achievements.

The last two prints of the Castiglione series take us back to the heart of Qing dynastic polity in the region of Peking – or Beijing, the Northern Capital. One depicts the ceremonial arrival of foreign vassal rulers and emissaries at the Forbidden City, the ritual and political centre of the empire and the main imperial residence as well as the heart of government. They enter by the main southern gate, which is easily recognisable as the place where today visitors buy tickets to enter the Palace Museum. In the print, the precinct below the gate towers is lined with hundreds if not thousands of men – officials and eunuchs – on parade to welcome the files of foreign visitors; today, each day, the same spot is populated by crowds of touts, hawkers and guides welcoming the tourists, both Chinese and foreign.

In the engravings of these military conquests, another scene is, if anything, even more important to the present story. It depicts a highly ritualised event of the emperor arriving at the dawn audience for visiting tribute-bearers and vassals. What may seem curious today is that this was also the basic and unvarying form of court etiquette for receiving foreigners: there was no facility for receiving emissaries of rulers on an equal footing to China, for none were considered as equals.

Unlike its counterpart in contemporary Europe, this Asian model of kingship did not involve the emperor vying for prestige with other monarchs on a world stage. It was assumed that China simply was the centre of the universe, as its Chinese name Zhongguo or 'Middle Kingdom' implies. Qing subjects were not permitted to leave China, but foreigners were welcome to come to be enlightened in China and to pay tribute – as vassals. If sincere, they would be sure to receive the emperor's condescension. Within the absolutist, hierarchical system of government in Qing China, this was the unquestioned world view.

It may, therefore, seem disconcerting that central to the image of the Emperor's temporary court is a vast rounded tent – an audience hall of a very particular kind. Although Qianlong was

emperor of China, he was ethnically a Manchu, and the tent
showed off the nomadic origins of his people on the Eurasian
steppe. All about are hills: this is clearly not a metropolitan scene
but one set a week's ride to the northeast of Peking and over the
Great Wall through the northern passes into the uplands of
Mongolia. This is Jehol in what used to be called Tartary, where
the Qianlong emperor moved the court to escape the summer
heat. It was here, among magnificent and extensive palace gardens
at Chengde in Jehol, that the emperor often held banquets[5] and
received foreign delegations including Lord Macartney's in 1793.
Macartney's draftsman, William Alexander, did not attend this
reception but made a drawing based on descriptions by his
colleagues – and possibly on engravings such as the one in the
Chester Beatty Library. **[figure 3]**

The drawing and the Chester Beatty Library print show the
iconography for such events: the emperor arrives from the left at
the head of a great column of officials, seated on a sedan chair
borne by thirty-two men. To the right, the foreign emissaries
stand to await the emperor's arrival.[6] From these two points, the
space recedes back into the image converging in European perspective along further lines of officials toward the great tent,
where the visitors will kowtow before the emperor and offer up
their tribute. The combination of a hybrid Sino-European style
with Qing imperial substance in this image is quite telling. At the
centre of the image is the Qing world-order and its sustaining
hierarchies and rituals.

This is the world into which King George III sent his emissary
Lord Macartney to negotiate an increase of Britain's exports to
China and establish diplomatic ties. It bears repeating that the
moving force behind the mission, and its financial backer, was the
East India Company or EIC – also known simply as 'the
Company' – and that China was perceived then, as now, as one
of the greatest untapped markets on earth.[7]

In the autumn of 1791, the EIC had little difficulty garnering
the support of the government, under William Pitt the Younger

(1759–1806), then Prime Minister (PM: 1783–1801, 1804–06), and Henry Dundas (1743–1811), the then Home Secretary. At this moment, the clear choice for ambassador was an individual with a glowing record as a diplomat and colonial administrator, the Antrim man George Macartney. A member of the Irish and British parliaments, Macartney had served as Governor of Grenada and Chief Secretary of Ireland. He had also distinguished himself as emissary to Catherine the Great (r. 1762–96) in St Petersburg, where he negotiated a trade treaty. Protracted discussions ensued between Macartney, his staff, various government departments and the Company, over salaries, conditions, goals and contributions. One of Macartney's conditions was that he be made an earl in the English aristocracy. When that could not be arranged immediately, he agreed to be made an Irish peer, Earl Macartney of Dervock, with his English earldom to follow.

In September 1792 the mission, comprising over 700 men, set sail in a squadron from Portsmouth. They would arrive in Peking almost a year later, in August 1793. For the ambassador and his suite, the Admiralty had provided *HMS Lion*, a 64-gun line-of-battle ship under Captain Sir Erasmus Gower. The EIC provided one of its roomiest and most comfortable ships for the transport of gifts for the emperor, the *Hindostan* (1300–1400 tons) under Captain Mackintosh, an experienced and respected Company officer. Also, two brigs, *Clarence* and *Jackal*, were to be in attendance through the Yellow Sea. Macartney had a major say in the selection of both the captains, who were known to him personally, and of his suite. Macartney's deputy was Sir George Staunton (1737–1801), who was to assume the position of ambassador in the event of Macartney's death.

After rounding the Cape of Good Hope, crossing the Indian Ocean and enjoying much hospitality through the Sunda Strait, the embassy touched at Macao. Local intelligence confirmed the earlier decision about how best to approach the emperor. This was to be on grounds of congratulating him on his eightieth birthday. For that reason, the embassy was permitted to proceed toward Peking by ship rather than taking the land route all across China. The next port of call was Zhoushan, near modern

Shanghai, where the East India Company wished to set up a trade entrepôt. Many of the sights along the way were recorded in official sketches by two appointed artists for the mission, as well as by several amateurs among the staff and crew.[8]

From Zhoushan the squadron proceeded north, around the Shandong peninsula, naming the landmarks and islands after members of the embassy and ships' officers, such as Cape Macartney and Cape Gower. Finally, the squadron headed north to the mouth of the White River, a place 120 miles south-east of Peking, where an official reception awaited. The embassy transferred into barges; Macartney turned a blind eye to the official banners declaring him to be a tribute envoy (although it might have given him some indication of how he was to be received). From here they were escorted upriver to the capital Peking and lodged in an imperial palace-garden complex, in the Garden of Perfect Clarity (Yuanmingyuan; also known as the Old Summer Palace), eight miles north-west of the imperial city. The two official artists for the mission, the Dublin portrait painter Thomas Hickey (1741–1824)[9] and William Alexander, remained here for weeks, even while Macartney himself moved into a comfortable town-house in the city, from where he was summoned up to the imperial summer residence at Chengde in Jehol, about 120 miles north-east of the capital, beyond the Great Wall.

One of Alexander's best sources among the ambassador's close staff must have been Captain Parish, an artillery officer and a fine amateur draftsman. His and others' sketches of Macartney's audience with the emperor were the basis for Alexander's later imaginary drawing of that event. Notably, this image records Macartney kneeling on one knee rather than kowtowing before the emperor. This was a staggering departure from normal Qing court protocol. Normally, all men – including ambassadors and foreign rulers – prostrated themselves and banged their heads on the ground before the emperor. Macartney had in fact won a major concession (see **figure 4** for a later caricature of this event by James Gillray). He was permitted to salute the emperor as he would his own sovereign – although Qianlong dismissed the idea that he would have his hand kissed.

As ambassador, Macartney's brief was to find ways to redress the growing trade deficit with China, which had come about in large part due to the fashion for the drinking of leaf tea. While happy to export tea, China failed to match this trade with corresponding imports of British goods, such as wool. In the new age of Adam Smith, such a trade imbalance was regarded as a grave concern, both by the East India Company and by its masters within the British Empire.

In fact, Macartney's diplomatic effort was ultimately pointless. The embassy had transported out to China a costly inventory of trade goods including scientific, optical and electrical instruments and machines, as well as the experts to reassemble and work them.[10] But these carefully selected objects the Qianlong emperor declared to be little more than curiosities. In addition, he stated that China had not the slightest need of any imports of British goods: 'Nevertheless,' he wrote in his second edict to George III, 'We do not forget the lonely remoteness of your island, cut off from the world by intervening wastes of sea, nor do We overlook your excusable ignorance of the usages of Our Celestial Empire.'[11]

In his first edict to King George, Qianlong had already spelled out his view of this foreign mission and its gifts: 'We have but one aim in view, namely, to maintain a perfect governance and to fulfil the duties of the state: strange and costly objects do not interest Us. If We have commanded that the tribute offerings sent by you, O King, are to be accepted, this was solely in consideration for the spirit which prompted you to dispatch them from afar. Our dynasty's majestic virtue has penetrated unto every country under heaven, and kings of all nations have offered their costly tribute by land and sea. As your Ambassador can see for himself, we possess all things. We set no value on objects strange or ingenious, and have no use for your country's manufactures.'

It seems that the emperor's dismissal of the embassy had been decided before Macartney had even landed; as had the refusal to consider any of the ambassador's requests regarding the expansion of trade and the establishment of a British diplomatic mission in Peking. The imperial edicts declared that, as there were no precedents, considering such requests was just too much trouble – impracticable and inconvenient. Today, many Chinese historians consider this episode to be an opportunity China missed to engage with the outside world – a failure of vision by an ageing absolute ruler and his court that laid their country bare to a century of imperialist aggression. The economic cost to China of the failure of Macartney's mission was worked out chiefly over the following century. British entrepreneurs found another drug to import forcibly into China: opium from Bengal, with its corrosive social effects. Meanwhile, they established a rival tea trade in India, which still flourishes.

For, although diplomatic channels had failed, the economic concerns remained. In the mid-nineteenth century the British Empire used naval power to enforce the import of opium into China during two Opium Wars and to negotiate what are still referred to as the 'humiliating treaties'. Yet from the available evidence in 1793, it seems that the Qianlong emperor and his court advisors had little idea of what they were dismissing or of the opportunity offered by Macartney's mission – and the strategic risks of rejecting it.

The document Macartney bore back to King George was an edict. Even though toned down in translation by missionaries, its condescending tone is unmistakable. In effect, its contempt for and ignorance of the niceties of international diplomacy balance the failure of the British mission to understand the predicament of Qing China under the ageing Qianlong emperor.

Immediately after its return home, although Macartney faced official censure, the story of his mission to China became a sensational topic of public interest. Illustrated reports and books by members of the embassy and its entourage soon appeared in print. The same appetite for news existed in France: despite the war between the two countries, declared during Macartney's outward journey to China, French editions also quickly emerged. From this period, it is to the deposed emperor of France, Napoleon Bonaparte (1769–1821), that the pithiest quote about China is attributed. In 1816, after his defeat at Waterloo and banishment to St Helena, he is believed to have said, '*Quand la Chine s'éveillera, le monde tremblera*' ('When China awakes, the world will tremble').

Today, China is awakening. Within the coming 'Chinese century', the failure of Macartney's mission stands as an admonition – for both China and the West – about the importance of remaining open, in pragmatic as well as ideological terms, each to the overtures of the other. Building cordial relations is not just about profit; it means learning to read the cultural cues as well.

.3.

An Irish Mandarin:

Sir Robert Hart in China 1854–1908

☆

RICHARD O'LEARY

Irish-born Sir Robert Hart (1835–1911) is widely regarded as the most influential foreigner in late nineteenth-century China. As Inspector-General of China's Maritime Customs Service he was a key figure in China's modernisation in the last decades of the Qing dynasty. Hart held an unusual post in that he was the foreign-born Inspector-General of an agency of the Chinese state. His position, combined with his almost permanent residency in China between 1854 and 1908, meant he was regularly consulted by both high officials in the Chinese (Qing) government and by officials of the foreign legations then in Beijing.

The function of the Maritime Customs Service was to regulate trading relations between China and the Western powers and to collect revenue for the Chinese government. From his appointment as Inspector-General in 1863, Hart built up the Customs Service over four decades into one of the most important bureaucracies of the Chinese state. By the end of the century the Customs Service was bringing in a quarter of the revenue available to the central Qing government. Under Hart the Customs Service also initiated a statistical service providing information on commodity markets and local trading networks, as well as facilitating participation in international exhibitions by a hitherto closed China. Also during this period, the customs postal service became a modern national postal service in China with 2,700 post offices. By 1906 Hart's staff included 11,970 persons, of whom 1,345 were foreigners. By an arrangement between the Chinese and Western powers, the staff in the higher levels of the service were almost all Westerners – as were its Inspectors-General.

Robert Hart was born on 20 February 1835 in Portadown, Co. Armagh. Middle class with a background in distilling, shopkeeping and farming, the Hart family later moved to Lisburn, Co. Down. There the young Hart spent a year at school in England before continuing his schooling at the Wesley Connexional School in Dublin. Robert Hart was only 15 years old when he went to study at Queen's College, Belfast (then one of the three Queen's Colleges in Ireland located at Belfast, Cork and Galway). He was a brilliant student, obtaining a Bachelor of Arts degree in 1853. On graduating, Hart was looking for a career and was willing to work abroad. In 1854 Queen's College Belfast successfully nominated him for a post in the British Consular Service as interpreter in China. With £100 for his passage, he set sail for China. Hart was 19 years old.

Hart's first appointment was to the British Consulate at Ningpo (Ningbo) and then to Canton (Guangzhuo). It is important to recall that, at the time, relatively little was known in the West about China. Few Westerners lived in the country and these were mainly traders and Christian missionaries who lived in the Treaty ports. Until shortly before Hart's arrival, China had been largely shut off from Western influences by a relatively inward-looking Qing imperial government.

China *and the* Irish

For this very reason, it is of immense interest that Hart kept a diary for most of his fifty-four years in China. In these journals, some of which have been transcribed and published, he shares with us some of his reflections on China, his own career and his personal life.[1] An entry in his journal in 1854 gives us a taste of his early experiences:

> Monday, 23 October 1854: 'Commenced my Chinese studies this morning; it is very strange at first to sit with a man who does not speak a word of English, and of whose language you are equally ignorant. I got the names of several objects from him and some two or three phrases. Some of his sounds remind me of the way you wd. speak to a horse.'[2]

Hart worked hard at successfully acquiring fluency in both the spoken and written Chinese language; he also displayed competency and suitable manners in dealing with Chinese officials. In 1859 he resigned from the British Consular Service to take up a post as Deputy Commissioner at Canton in the expanding Chinese Maritime Customs. It is clear that Hart benefited from changes during what proved to be a period of political turmoil and administrative restructuring. This, combined with his proven abilities and fluency in Chinese, resulted in his appointment in 1863 as Inspector-General of the Customs. He was 28 years old. Hart's career as Inspector-General of the Customs was to become his life: he was to spend the next 45 years in China, apart from two periods of leave in 1866 and 1878.

In 1866 Hart returned to Ireland with a view to finding a wife. There he married Hester Bredon, the daughter of his family doctor in Portadown. Hester returned with him to China where they had three children. [**figure 5**] However, Hessie left China in 1882 to settle down permanently in England with their children. The couple did not see each other again until 24 years later, in 1906, although they continued to communicate amicably and very frequently by post.

Hart in China lived through the Taiping Rebellion of the 1850s and early 1860s and a number of foreign invasions. But the most dramatic and dangerous event was the Boxer Rebellion: a violently anti-foreign and anti-Christian movement which emerged in 1898, resulting in many foreigners as well as Chinese being killed. Railway lines were ripped up and eventually, when all telegraph communication ceased, Beijing was isolated from the international world. In the summer of 1900, Hart was one of the many foreigners besieged by the Boxers in the foreign legations in Beijing. Hart's death, with obituary, was prematurely reported in the 17 July edition of the London *Times* newspaper. The Customs offices, his house and all his property were destroyed in the rebellion.

That same year the rebellion was suppressed by Western military intervention and Hart was able to resume his work at the Customs Service until 1908. By the time of his retirement, Hart had received many honours from both the Chinese government (his employer) and Western governments. These honours included:

> *The Peacock's Feather* (1885) and *The Ancestral Rank of the First Class of the First Order for Three Generations* (1889) from China;

> *KCMG* (1882), *GCMG* (1889) and a *Baronetcy* (1993) from the United Kingdom;

> A grand officer of the *Legion d'honneur* (1885) from France;

> *Commander of the Order of Pius IX* (1885) from the Holy See, Rome (quite an achievement for Hart as an Ulster Protestant!).

These awards reflected the many services Hart had provided in mediating between the West and China. For, as Inspector-General, Hart wielded considerable power and influence, often negotiating on behalf of the Chinese with both European and American authorities. In this role, it has been suggested that Hart occupied a nodal point in a network of transnational élites (comprising leading diplomats, merchants, bankers, journalists and academics) that emerged during the nineteenth century as commercial exchanges intensified and international contacts broadened.[3] Other historians have written of Hart that 'No single foreigner in nineteenth-century China had more sustained influence than Hart, and none enjoyed a greater measure of Chinese confidence.'[4] At one time or another, his advice was sought on fiscal matters, railways, foreign relations and national defense. This raises the question of what characteristics and experiences enabled Hart to work so successfully with both Chinese and Western officials.

The editors of Hart's journals, Bruner, Fairbank and Smith, refer to what they call Hart's 'bi-cultural achievement' in being able to straddle cultures and win the confidence of his Chinese overseers by adapting so successfully to Chinese cultural and behavioural expectations. In Hart, they detect a trait of cultural sensitivity unusual among the foreign merchants of the Treaty ports in China. Hart was a sharp observer of cultural differences: he paid great attention to Chinese rules of protocol and courtesy. Another commentator emphasises Hart's success in cultivating personal relationships with senior officials in the Zongli Yamen (Qing department of Foreign Affairs), including Prince Gong (1833–1898) – relationships which were mutually beneficial.[5]

If we look more closely into Hart's private life we find even more intimate relationships with the Chinese. Hart formed a relationship with a Chinese woman, Ayaou, between 1857 and about 1864, from which were born three children. This relationship – of Western men keeping a Chinese sexual partner – was more than the common custom in the mid-nineteenth century (when there were few available Western women in China). In 1866 the connection was dissolved and Ayaou was then presented with $3,000 when she surrendered the children to Hart's agent and herself married a Chinaman. The children – Anna, Herbert and Arthur – were sent to England where it was arranged that Hart's lawyer would take charge of them as Hart's wards. Hart provided for them financially, although he never saw them again. In the view of the two women academics who have examined this, Hart was kind to his wards but he was also rational and determined to prevent it from interfering with either his later married life with Hessie or his career in the Customs.[6] In the view of his journal editors, 'By the standards of the day such behaviour was generous in the extreme' as 'many Westerners simply ignored and abandoned such children'.[7]

And what about the Western background that Hart brought to his engagement with China? In the obituary of him published prematurely in the London *Times* (17 July 1900), the Customs Service was described as 'one of the most striking monuments ever produced by the genius and labour of any individual Englishman'. Here Hart was described as English, despite the fact that the Irish-born Hart had spent remarkably little time in England – one year in a boarding school and short visits during his two return trips to Europe in 1866 and 1878. This is in contrast with his 18 years in Ireland, most of it in Ulster. Readers from Ireland are well used to such English acquisitions of the Irish-born (and, of course, to do them justice, Hart's part of Ireland was then, and remains, part of the United Kingdom. Even today, Hart would have identified himself initially as a British citizen). More importantly perhaps, Hart, depending on the context, refers to himself in terms of being British, Irish, an Ulsterman and sometimes even English. Such subtle distinctions carry significance in Ireland although they are more difficult for the Chinese to grasp; certainly at the time, the primary distinction would have been simply between Chinese and foreigners.

Irish-born employees were recorded (correctly) as British citizens by the Chinese Customs. Furthermore, Hart is not always consistent in his own use of the terms 'British' and 'English'. Sometimes he uses the term 'the English' to refer to the British administration. This is evident in the following extract from a letter to James Campbell, the customs secretary in England, where his political sympathy with Britain also shines through: 'You know that I have been trying these last twenty five years to keep military and naval appointments in China, if not in English hands, at least from going into hands likely to exert an influence hostile to English interests, and in that way likely to work badly for China in the long run.'[8] We note here that he does not see English/British and Chinese interests as incompatible. This is important as there are divergent historical assessments of Hart – ranging from a defensive insistence that he aided China to claims that he advanced British imperialism. Hart for his part appeared genuinely to believe that British and Qing interests overlapped in many areas.

Hart comments on occasions on the English in a reflective way which indicates that culturally he is not thoroughly of that group. He wrote in 1893 to Campbell (another Briton): 'I am not in favour of bringing out any experienced English hand: English are not properly accommodating and they have not enough India-rubber in their composition, and for success native wants and native conditions must be studied and allowed for – too parishional, too provincial, too insular are our countrymen!'[9]

As may be seen from these comments, Hart had a liberal commitment to cosmopolitanism. He was also able to rise above his own provincial and insular background and his own social origins, which in terms of his peripheral place of birth in Ireland, middle-class background and nonconformist religion all lay outside the heart of the English upper-class Anglican establishment. These factors may have honed his skills of cultural sensitivity and accommodation.

One sinologist, Jonathan Spence, highlights the ambiguity of Hart's position, which involved his fending off criticisms of merchants and even consuls that he favoured Chinese over British interests while enduring the opposite suspicion from the Chinese.[10] **[see figure 6]** Spence suggests that Hart's regularly expressed desire to return home was an attempt to keep his identity assured. In any case, the fact that he was not English-born may have added a different complexity to these divided loyalties. Hart in China remembered and celebrated the national holidays of the British Queen's birthday, the Irish national day of St Patrick's Day, as well as the Ulster Protestant holiday of the

Twelfth of July. Of course, it might be argued that, in the period Hart lived in Ireland, it was easier to hold multiple British and Irish identities than it was to become in the later nineteenth and the twentieth centuries. During this time, violent political conflict in Ireland and later in Northern Ireland resulted in a greater polarisation between British and Irish identities.

Having retrieved Hart from a simple British identity, we might wish to reintroduce him as the forgotten Irishman. In his journal entries and letters, Hart regularly refers to his Ulster or Irish origin and identity. For Stanley Wright, Hart's main biographer, Hart was all his life proud of his Irish origins and he himself saw little conflict between his multiple identities.[11]

In Hart's own diaries there are several references to an Irish identity. In his first year in China he wrote: 'I'm an Irishman – a Paddy in heart and soul,' although he adds 'and yet it was without a sigh that I left my native land …'[12] Another early entry: 'Here I think about home and friends and acquaintances and "Fatherland" or as some prefer "Mother Country". It is Tea Time with all the Middle Classes: it is a joyous hour throughout "Ould Ireland".'[13] Note the emphasis on missed friends and acquaintances, which were arguably more important to Hart than place.

Again, Hart wrote to a fellow Irishman and colleague in China, Patrick J. Hughes, that 'In these "why and wheresome" days, I wonder how you could take it for granted that I drowned my shamrock in orthodox Hibernian fashion on Patrick's Day. It was certainly to be expected that that exiled Paddies like you and me would keep up the good old national custom, but "shame on me", I forgot all about the matter … it quite escaped my memory.'[14] On occasions, when he meets other Irishmen, Hart notes in his diaries or letters their common Irishness, in a way that he does not do in encounters with English persons. It was also reported that in conversation his Chinese displayed an Irish accent.

Moreover, it is well documented that, throughout his life, Hart wrote very regularly to his family and other connections in Ireland. His life-long connection with his former university, Queen's College, Belfast, was particularly strong. On his death, his wife wrote in 1911 to the Vice-Chancellor of Queen's that 'he loved the University, and took an interest in it, second only to his Chinese official work; he felt he owed his start in life to it'.[15] His interest is evident in a journal entry in China – nine years after he graduated – reporting that 'Brown and Watters dined with me in the evening, and we had gossip about Belfast and College people.'[16] Twenty-six years after graduating, he sent a donation for the testimonial of one of his former professors. In 1882 Queen's made him an honorary Doctor of Law. On his retirement from China his attachment to Queen's was evident by his appointment (1908–11) as Pro-Chancellor to the university.

Hart never forgot or lost contact with Ireland, reflecting that 'I suppose it is the same with all who go far from home and work in foreign lands: we never forget, and a sound, or a smell, brings up cradle days and all the surroundings of Home Sweet Home.'[17] However, care must be taken to recognise the limits to Hart's Irish identity. There is no doubt that Hart at times described himself as an Irishman, just as he referred to himself at times as British, as an Ulsterman and sometimes even as English. Indeed these multiple aspects of identity could be said to indicate that Hart's culture was already multifaceted even before he came to China (where he supposedly achieved the claimed 'bi-culturality'). Obviously, the incorporation of Chinese culture was a much wider cultural addition. But the point being made is that it is unhelpful to view Hart as a monocultural person who subsequently became engaged with 'Chinese' culture. As is clear from the above, Hart was never monocultural, nor did he perceive himself as such.

What can also be said is that Hart himself explicitly recognised that the Irish dimension of his cultural background was something on which he could usefully draw, in at least one specific kind of encounter. 'The Chinese respect the man who can drink much,' Hart wrote. 'If I had known this at the time I should have surprised them. Who can boast of a stronger head in this respect than an Irishman?'[18] But it should also be added that this sociability based on alcohol, which Hart participated in, was far removed from the abstinence associated with the Methodist faith of his youth.

What is of additional interest is the question of whether Hart fostered close relations with other important Irish-born figures in China. Among other highly influential Irish-born in China in this period were Sir John Newell Jordan (1852–1925) and Sir Thomas Jackson (1841–1915). Jordan's career displayed remarkable parallels with that of Hart. Ulster-born Jordan graduated from Queen's College (in 1873) and three years later entered the British Consular service as a student interpreter in China. By 1891 he rose through the ranks to the post of Chinese Secretary. Jackson, like Hart, was from County Armagh and progressed to become chief executive of the Hong Kong and Shanghai Bank (HSBC), one of the banks with which both the Chinese Custom Service and Hart personally did business. At the very least their common Ulster-Irish backgrounds may have facilitated the ease of communication between Hart and Jordan and the British administration and between Hart and Jackson and the HSBC.[19]

There are other examples of Hart's Irish connections in China which may be even more significant. In 1885, during the period of tense diplomatic relations between Britain, France and China concerning Burma, Hart was consulted by both the British and Chinese governments and acted as something of a mediator. During a period of intense consultations, Hart met the head of the British legation at Beijing, Nicholas O'Conor, on an almost daily basis. Hart also communicated regularly on the matter with Lord Dufferin, the Viceroy of India. These three men were pivotal to the delicate negotiations between the British and Chinese governments, and all three were of Irish origin. O'Conor was born in 1843 in County Roscommon and Dufferin was a son of the Blackwood family from County Down in Ulster and succeeded to an Irish peerage.

Hart remarked in a letter to Campbell at the time of the Burma crisis: 'No sooner out of the France-Tonking affair than we have the England-Burmah complication to deal with. I would rather not touch it … but the Prince … asks me to arrive at a friendly understanding without running the risk of an official rupture in an official channel. Fortunately, O'Conor and myself are good friends.'[20]

China *and the* Irish

Like his fellow Irish-born O'Conor and Dufferin, Hart believed that British administration could enable both economic and political development; clearly this affected his views of that administration, whether in China or in Ireland. Hart opposed Irish nationalism on the grounds that British rule was good for Ireland. This is not unlike his argument for the British presence in China, that it was good for China. Here may also be an instance where we can point to the difference deriving from being an Irish-born, as opposed to an English-born, citizen of what was then the United Kingdom of Great Britain and Ireland. For an Englishman, British rule in his own country is not problematic and he may rarely be asked to defend it. However, in Ireland, British rule was contested – and Hart was part of a minority section of the Irish population who had to make the argument for Britain's continuing rule in Ireland. Being in this position may have made Hart, and the Irish in China who supported Britain, better equipped to understand and engage with the critics of British administration.

As regards the question of Irish Home Rule, Hart was – as were the great majority of Ulster Protestants – a Unionist, but he was still able to maintain a sense of both an Ulster and an Irish identity. This is evident in a letter he wrote to the Association of Ulstermen in London in 1909, thanking them for making him their guest at a banquet. As he wrote after that occasion: 'I had excellent seconding in the very able and cosmopolitan staff of both Chinese and foreigners at my disposal and among that staff I had Irishmen from various districts and several Ulstermen who always satisfied their chief and did credit for the land they came from – the Ireland we all love.'[21] It is in this issue of recruitment of fellow Irishmen that Hart's true favoritism towards the Irish becomes most evident.

The editors of Hart's journals describe Hart's Irish-born nepotism as every bit as strong as the Chinese examples he saw about him. Indeed they point out that the concern with family ties was part of his Irish cultural background and that this emphasis on family was something he shared with the Chinese. Eight members of Hart's family joined the Chinese Customs – a brother, two brothers-in-law, his son and three nephews. His family members achieved senior positions within the organisation. On his retirement, Hart endeavoured to be succeeded by his brother and his brother-in-law, Robert Bredon; and indeed later his nephew, Frederick William Maze, did eventually become Inspector-General. The charge of nepotism remains significant as it relates not just to Hart's personality but also on how it reflects on the Custom Service's aspiration to be a modern, multinational, meritocratic institution. Hart was well aware of the favouritism he exercised towards his own family but declared that 'I have never advanced a worse man over a better; yet, if promotion is due to one of two men of equal deserts, and one of them is my own flesh and blood, it would simply be unnatural to pass him over.'[22]

In his defence it may be argued that nepotism was at least tempered by considerations of ability. In fact, Hart did refuse employment to some of his relatives – notably his brother-in-law James Maze and his two country cousins. He described this brother-in-law as unsuitable. The cousins did not pass the qualifying exam set in London by Campbell.

What was more significant numerically than family members was the recruitment into the Customs of a disproportionate number of other persons from Ireland. Hart drew these from a variety of sources, including his old college. Hart himself had been recruited from Queen's College, Belfast, and continued to take an interest in his old university, so we should not be too surprised that he should sometimes have deliberately recruited graduates from the Queen's Colleges, especially from Belfast and Cork (now University College Cork). For example, in 1881 he wrote two letters to Professors Purser and Canning, asking them to send him four Queen's College men as Medical Officers and Assistants.[23]

Hart also remembered childhood and school friendships from Ireland and England. For example, in 1889 he provided a nomination for Evans – the nephew of a schoolmate who had been with Hart at the Connexional School in Dublin in 1847–1850. A theme which runs through Hart's behaviour is what we might call the 'auld lang syne' factor. This song with its lyrics 'Should auld acquaintance be forgot' was a favorite of Hart's. Indeed on more than one occasion he explicitly provided it as a reason for his actions. He wrote to Campbell, 'I promised his second son an appointment … I wish to oblige Winchester in this matter for "auld lang syne".'[24] It captures something personal of Hart, the man, reflecting both his view of his country of origin and his favouritism towards old acquaintances in matters of recruitment.

In addition to recruitment from childhood or college friendships, other persons favoured tended to be from Ulster and Ireland. Although he had emigrated from Ulster in the 1850s and was himself of only middle-class origins, by the 1870s and 1880s Hart had formed social ties with some of Ulster's most prominent families, such as the Montgomerys and the Warings from County Down. These were old Ulster landed gentry families, and in addition Thomas Waring was a Member of Parliament. These connections offered more than social status as they could provide additional links to the British social and political establishment. Nor were the benefits of the association operating only one way. In 1876 a son of Hugh Montgomery had joined the Customs Service and would eventually attain the rank of Commissioner.[25] Requests to Hart for nominations to the Customs Service need not be seen as simply a kindness to old acquaintances or a pressure which came with high office: they also presented Hart with an opportunity to enhance his and his family's social status back in Ireland and England.

In conclusion, Hart and the Customs Service stood at the interface between China and the West at a critical time, allowing Hart to play a significant role in the modernisation of China. For his own part, Hart appeared genuinely to believe that he served China's interests and that there was no conflict between the two nations he served, as British and Chinese interests overlapped in many areas. Today, in an independent Ireland, whose nationalists have emphasised the negative aspects of British colonial rule, there are difficulties in reclaiming Hart as Irish: for it requires his countrymen to acknowledge that many born in Ireland were also significant actors in Britain's role in China. But, as has been argued here, Hart held, and was comfortable with, multiple and overlapping identities, both Irish and British, and this may even have assisted him in successfully leading the multinational organisation that was the Chinese Customs Service as well as with dealing with officials from many different governments.

Thus Robert Hart's significance is undeniable and his abilities are irrefutable. In addition, his commitment of most of his life to working in China, his relatively generous treatment of his Chinese partner and children and his degree of awareness of Chinese culture all show an unusual level of attachment by a Westerner to his adopted country of China.

.4.

From Patsy O'Wang to Fu Manchu:

Ireland, China and Racism

✦

FINTAN O'TOOLE

In the Hollywood western *Seraphim Falls*, Pierce Brosnan, with Liam Neeson in close pursuit, rides into a railroad construction camp. As the wide shot closes in, we see the workers laying the rails, Chinese men in wide-brimmed straw hats on one side, Irish navvies on the other. As Brosnan moves through the camp, the images are a series of visual clichés. The Chinese look at him silently, impassively and of course inscrutably. The first close-up shots of the Irishmen are of a small group playing cards with a bottle of whiskey between them on the makeshift table. The next is of a man drinking from a hip flask. We cut back to more anonymous Chinese and Irish navvies laying a rail and hammering spikes. Then we're back again to a red-haired Irishman stealing Brosnan's liquor, as the star mutters sardonically,

'Help yourself, Paddy boy.' In the one moment when one of the Chinese gets to speak, he says something unintelligible in his own language and Brosnan's only reply is to smash him in the face and push him aside.

Seraphim Falls was released in 2007, yet its images of Chinese and Irish workers would not have been out of place in the late-nineteenth century. This scene in the railroad camp encapsulates both a historical reality and the way that reality has been frozen into a set of stereotypes. On the one hand, it reminds us that something we take to be a new Irish experience – the way we now mingle with Chinese people in our ordinary mundane existence – is not so new after all. On the other, it hints at the reasons why that reality has so little purchase on our contemporary sense of Irish identity. It exists, not as lived history, but as a clichéd background to a whole other drama – the emergence of the United States as a global superpower. If we want to place the current encounters of the Irish and the Chinese in their actual historical context, we have to disentangle that history from the mythology in which it is embedded.

The building of the first transcontinental railway, linking the Atlantic and Pacific coasts of the United States, is one of the key moments in the emergence of global modernity. It symbolically reunited the US after its bitter civil war, ensured the final defeat of the American Indians, opened up the West to new waves of European migration and laid the basis for America's subsequent triumph as the world's dominant power. It was completed on 10 May 1869, when the rails of the Union Pacific – reaching westward from Omaha, Nebraska – and those of the Central Pacific Railroad – reaching eastward from Sacramento, California – were joined, completing the coast-to-coast connection.

That mythic moment was preceded a little over a week earlier by another vividly symbolic episode, when the might of American industry was demonstrated by the laying of ten miles of railroad on a single day. That track was actually laid by just eight Irishmen – George Elliott, Edward Killeen, Thomas Daley, Mike Shaw, Mike Sullivan, Mike Kennedy, Fred McNamara and Patrick Joyce. Most of the workers who prepared the ground, hauled the materials and assisted the Irish rail-handlers were

Chinese migrants from Canton (Guangdong). This was entirely appropriate because the bulk of the manpower that built the track from coast to coast was Chinese and Irish. This seminal event in the creation of the world we now inhabit was, at ground level, essentially a joint Chinese–Irish enterprise. When the ceremonial last spike was driven, the crowd that gathered around to witness the moment was a mongrel gathering in which the Irish and the Chinese were most prominent. As the engineer Amos Bowsher, who was present, recalled: 'It was certainly a cosmopolitan gathering. Irish and Chinese labourers, who had set records in tracklaying that have never since been equalled, joined with the cowboys, Mormons, miners and Indians in celebrating completion of the railroad.'[1] **[figure 7]** Yet, instead of being remembered as heroes of modernity, those Chinese and Irish workers linger, if they remain in the memory at all, only as the stereotypes of *Seraphim Falls* – inscrutable Chinamen and drunken, thieving Irishmen.

As Stanley Aronowitz has put it, 'The Irish and Chinese constituted the first genuine American proletariat. They were propertyless in the historical sense of possessing neither capital nor land, as well as in the modern sense of possessing no skills that would give them status within the industrial system.'[2] This shared economic status meant that nineteenth-century Irish and Chinese migrants tended to be bracketed together in the set of interlocking stereotypes that defined foreigners for the Anglo-American mainstream: the Chinese talked funny, ate strange things and wore pigtails; the Irish had brogues, drank whiskey and fought. Both were characterised as deviating, albeit in opposite directions, from the supposed Anglo-Saxon norm of level-headed stability. The Chinese were stereotyped as being naturally slavish, lacking the independent spirit of the proper white male. The Irish, on the other hand, were impossibly unruly, lacking the discipline of the civilised urban man. One ethnic group was too obedient, the other not obedient enough. But, though the stereotypes occupied two distant poles, they amount to the same thing – a sub-human inferiority.

In the cartoons of Joseph Keppler and Thomas Nast, the Irish and the Chinese were represented in the same ape-like way. Keppler's and Nast's 'Chinese were drawn with high cheekbones and chimpanzee mouths, while their Irish were drawn in classic Anglo-American fashion, with square-jawed, large-nostrilled, gorilla faces'.[3] If anything, the Chinese chimps were slightly above the Irish gorillas on the evolutionary scale. An 1880 set of cartoons by Joseph Keppler for *Puck* magazine shows the Chinese displacing the Irish in New York, taking their jobs and beating them up. A volunteer Chinese fire company is shown washing the city clean of Mayor John Kelley, the successor to Boss Tweed, and of the corruption of the Irish-dominated Tammany Hall.

Conversely, for a Chinese man to become Irish was a retrograde step. In Thomas Stewart Denison's play of 1895, *Patsy O'Wang: an Irish Farce with a Chinese Mix-up*, Chin Sum, a docile and obedient Chinese cook working for an American scientist, Dr Fluke, accidentally drinks from a bottle of what he thinks is brandy but that actually contains 'spirit of Hibernia'. It releases his dark inner self – he has an Irish father, whose latent genetic heritage now becomes open. Chin Sum is transformed into Patsy O'Wang. As Denison's notes explain: 'Whiskey, the drink of his father, transforms him into a true Irishman, while strong tea, the beverage of his mother, has the power of restoring fully his Chinese character.'

Much to his employer's disgust, Patsy declares that he is now 'Irish forever' and becomes wild and troublesome. 'I'm going into politics. Me ambition is to be alderman and die beloved and respected by all.' The play ends with him singing:

Me father was Hooligan, me mother was Chinay
And I was born in Hong Kong town ten thousand miles away ...
One day I brewed the punch meself and then I tried the same –
Hooray, it touched a vital spot, it lit the Irish flame.[4]

This transformation of Chinese to Irish could also work the other way round in mainstream American imagery. Twenty-five years earlier in his satiric squib *John Chinaman in New York*, Mark Twain described an encounter with a Chinese man holding a sign outside a tea store. Seeing passers-by stare at the man, he wrote, 'I pitied the friendless Mongol' with his 'quaint Chinese hat with peaked roof and ball on top, and his long queue dangling down his back; his short silken blouse …'. Twain wonders 'what was passing behind his sad face, and what distant scene his vacant eye was dreaming of. Were his thoughts with his heart, ten thousand miles away, beyond the billowy wastes of the Pacific? among the ricefields and the plumy palms of China? under the shadows of remembered mountain peaks, or in groves of bloomy shrubs and strange forest trees unknown to climes like ours? A cruel fate it is, I said, that has befallen this bronzed warrior.'

He touches the man on the shoulder in sympathy and promises him that 'Money shall be raised – you shall go back to China – you shall see your friends again.' He asks him what wages he's paid. '"Divil a cent," says the man, "but four dollars a week … but it's aisy, barrin' the troublesome furrin clothes that's so expensive."'[5]

This odd coupling of the Chinese and the Irish reflected the tensions and prejudices of nineteenth-century America. But it had its roots in an even stranger intellectual conceit, one that arose much closer to home. This was the idea that the peculiarity of the Irish, their inability to conform to 'civilised' European norms, could be explained by the fact that they were not really Europeans at all. Embedded in the Tudor colonial conquest of Ireland was the notion that the natives were not proper Westerners but an Eastern people who had ended up in the wrong place. The English ideologues imagined that the Wild Irish must really derive from the prototypical barbarians, the nomadic Scythians of the Eurasian steppes. In *A View of the Present State of Ireland* (1596) Edmund Spenser concluded that the Irish were made up of many races but that 'the chiefest … I suppose to be Scythians'.[6] Likewise, his contemporary Fynes Moryson reported that 'the Gangaui, a Scithean people comming into Spaine, and from thence into Ireland, inhabited the county of Kerry'.[7]

This notion was revived in the eighteenth century, with Scythians, Mongols and Chinese all serving interchangeably as the Eastern race from which the Irish were derived. The Scottish philologist David Malcolm decided in the mid-eighteenth century that the inhabitants of St Kilda spoke an ancient form of Irish that still showed the marks of its Chinese origins.[8] In 1818, Charles Vallancey argued that the Chinese and the Irish were both descended from the Scythians and proved this by showing, as he thought, 'the origin of the ancient Celts and their language from the Orientals'.[9]

Mad as this idea was, it proved very hard to dislodge. English travellers compared the cabins of Chinese and Irish peasants and the mourning songs of Chinese women to Irish keening. The discovery in the late eighteenth and early nineteenth centuries, in various parts of Ireland, of over a hundred small porcelain seals with Chinese characters inscribed on them seemed to prove the link. Once the notion was in the air, it attached itself to all sorts of speculations. In *Thoughts on the Moral Order of Nature*, published in Dublin in 1831, Anna Maria Winter writes that 'I never, certainly, heard of any likeness being traced between the Chinese and the Irish character, but yet I think it likely that, whenever those peculiarities of natural disposition which distinguish one nation from another, have been fully investigated, it will be found that the Irish character is, fundamentally, an European one, with a Chinese superstructure, and that it is owing to this remarkable combination that, whether you travel from Europe to China by the East or by the West, you still find people who, in their character, have a likeness to the Irish.'

The connection was not, in general, flattering to the Irish, who were seen as a decadent vestige of Chinese civilisation. In 1844, on the eve of the Great Famine, the royal physician, James Johnson, reporting on his tour of Ireland, writes that 'If the Chinese had possession of ERIN, they would soon convert it into a "Celestial Empire", to which title it certainly has little claim at present. We should then see "Paddy" flourish on the slopes and summits of every mountain, from Carran Tual to Carrantagher, instead of burrowing in earth-holes, inhaling smoke, and crunching the bones of potatoes; while the water-tanks of the Atlantic clouds would irrigate the rice-fields in "illigant style."'[10]

China *and the* Irish

Faced with this notion that they were like the Chinese – only worse – the Irish who actually came into contact with real Chinese people responded in varied, and indeed contradictory, ways. In America, they competed with Chinese labourers at the bottom of the economic heap. Sometimes, they sought an advantage by appealing to white, Christian solidarity against the Heathen Chinee. In San Francisco, the Cork-born labour leader Denis Kearney, aided by his sidekick C.C. O'Donnell, formed the Workingmen's Party of California in 1877, held anti-Chinese rallies and began and ended every speech with the slogan 'The Chinese must go!' **[figure 8]** Kearney blamed unemployment among white workers on the supposed slave mentality of Chinese workers, who had come to California looking for work after the completion of the transcontinental railroad and who, he claimed, were willing to accept lower pay and worse conditions. He claimed that corporations went as far as China to recruit workers because it was easier to control them 'as serfs'. Their character, he maintained, predisposed them to obedience. 'They are whipped curs, abject in docility, mean, contemptible and obedient in all things. They have no wives, children or families … they seem to have no sex.'[11] Kearney's manipulation of these deeply entrenched stereotypes of the Chinese fomented anti-Chinese riots in California, led to the passage of a series of discriminatory laws in the state and ultimately fed into the passage at federal level of a ban, through the Chinese Exclusion Act of 1882, on further Chinese immigration to the United States.

What Kearney did with shocking success was to accept the stereotypical dichotomy between Chinese docility and Irish wildness, turn it into a racially charged opposition between a slave mentality and a proud spirit and then use it to elevate Irish and other European workers over their Chinese counterparts. **[figure 9]**

In the cultural sphere, there was a similar way for the Irish to deal with the convoluted intertwining of their own image and that of the Chinese migrants: by manufacturing anti-Chinese carica-tures of their own. The great Irish vaudevillian Edward Harrigan, one of the inventors of Broadway theatre, created the lustful, thieving, opium-smoking Hog-Eye, whose antagonistic relation-ship with the Irish washerwoman Honora Dublin reflects real competition between Irish women and Chinese men in the laundry business and for jobs in domestic service. In *The Mulligans' Silver Wedding*, written in 1881, Honora Dublin launches a viciously racist tirade, significantly in a quarrel over a clothes line, against Hog-Eye: 'You're not half a man. You're a nagur, you eat your dinner with drumsticks. You're a monkey, you have a tail growing out of your head. You're a mongrel Asiatic … Why don't you have whiskers on your face like a man, you baboon you …The likes of you coming to a free country and walking around in your petticoats and calling yourself a man …'.[12] This stream of abuse, with its explicit feminisation of the Chinese enemy, picks up directly on Kearney's notion of the Chinese as sexless creatures. Hog-Eye, as John Kuo Wei Tchen has put it, 'was the heathen's heathen, the Irish other's other'.[13]

The quintessential embodiment of the Yellow Peril in twentieth-century Western popular culture, the evil Dr Fu Manchu – who plots to take over the world for the Chinese race – was also a largely Irish creation. He was invented by Sax Rohmer, really the Irishman Arthur Ward whose *nom de plume* was partly derived from the Irish hero Patrick Sarsfield. Fu Manchu and his successor Sin Fang were played in dozens of films by the Irish actor Harry Agar Lyons. The evil genius was drawn for the popular American newspaper strip cartoon by the Irish-American artist Leo O'Mealia.

There were more positive images of China and the Chinese in Irish writing, such as Oscar Wilde's appreciation of the ancient philosopher Chuang Tsu and Eugene O'Neill's use of China in his play *Marco Millions* as the epitome of genuine civilisation, as con-trasted with the grasping narrowness of the West. But in terms of their impact on popular consciousness, Hog-Eye and Fu Manchu are undoubtedly the most important Irish contributions to the representation of the Chinese in the West, and they form the most disreputable strand of Irish–Chinese relations. Yet the very virulence of Honora Dublin's attack on Hog-Eye should alert us to the fact that something else is going on here. It draws attention to the reality that, in the nineteenth century, there was a very good chance that Honora Dublin and Hog-Eye might not have been mortal enemies at all. They might, in fact, have been man and wife. In fact, Mrs Dublin's tirade in *The Mulligans' Silver Wedding* is partly sparked by a proposal of marriage. Hog-Eye, in Harrigan's caricature of Chinese speech, tells her, 'Me likee you. Makee velly goodee wifee … Miss-ee Hog-Eye.' In reality, not all Irish women reacted to such proposals with Mrs Dublin's vile outrage.

The great secret of Irish–Chinese relations is that, with striking frequency, Irish women in the diaspora married Chinese men. Irish women often migrated alone, without their families, and sometimes greatly outnumbered the Irish male population of host communities. Chinese migration to America and Australia, conversely, was disproportionately made up of single men. For significant numbers of Irish women, these relatively sober, hard-working Chinese men made attractive husbands.

In 1860, for example, the *Quarterly Review* in London, reporting on the gold rush in Ballarat in Australia, notes that 'There are several wealthy Chinese merchants in [Melbourne], who have large transactions with their countrymen on the different gold-fields. Few women accompany them, but they are said to succeed in obtaining wives among the Irish.'[14]

At the same time in New York there was already a well-established enclave of Chinese men married to or living with Irish women around James Street, south of Chatham Square. As early as 1857, *Harper's Weekly* was noting marriages between Chinese cigar vendors and Irish apple peddlers in the city, claiming that 28 of the latter had recently 'gone the way of matrimony with their elephant-eyed, olive-skinned contemporaries'.[15] By the end of the decade, the *New York Times* noted that most owners of Chinese boarding houses were married to either Irish or German women. Shop windows displayed mechanical toys of Chinese men dancing with Irish women. In March 1858, *Yankee Notions* ran a cartoon on its cover of a Chinese–Irish couple with the Irish woman telling their children: 'Now, then, Chang-Mike, run home and take Pat-Chow and Rooney-Sing wid ye, and bring the last of the puppy pie for yer daddy. And, do ye mind? bring some praties for yer mother, ye spalpeens. (To her husband) How be's ye, Chang-Honey?'[16] **[figure 10]**

This caricature represented a genuine phenomenon: by the late 1870s, a quarter of all Chinese men in New York city were married to Irish women. By 1882, the *New York Sun* could report that the Chinese 'from the fashionable clubs of Mott and Park Street rode ... in Chatham Square coaches, carrying a Liberal supply of liquor and cigars ... accompanied by their Irish wives, many of them young, buxom and attractive.' These men were often seen as good catches by their Irish wives. A writer for the *Sun* described his visit to a Chinese clubhouse and his exchange with a 'young and pretty Irish girl, scarcely over eighteen': "Today we had a nice dinner, chickens and such things, and the men and their wives are now smoking and drinking sour wine. The wives are all Irish girls. I'm married." "What, married to a Chinaman?" "Certainly," she answered proudly, "married two weeks today." Then laughing outright she went on to say that the Chinamen were all good "fellows", that they work hard, go to night school, and are devoted to their wives.'[17]

These marriages produced offspring, but those children do not figure in our notions of Irish America. It is much more likely that their descendants are counted now as Asian Americans. The irony is that whereas the mainstream racism of the nineteenth century tended to place the Irish and the Chinese in close imaginative proximity, the second wave of globalisation in the twentieth century set them apart. The situation of twenty-first-century Ireland, in which significant inward Chinese migration is again creating the prospect of a mixed Chinese–Irish identity, thus seems new and confusing. It does so because its earlier history has been occluded. That history survives only in the arid stereotypes that we glimpse in *Seraphim Falls*. The more interesting and complex reality to which those stereotypes related has been lost.

Yet Ireland's history as an emigrant society means that few kinds of cross-cultural encounter can ever be really new to us. There is already a complex human legacy on which we can draw. It is striking, for example, that a collection of autobiographical reflections by bi-racial and bi-cultural writers in America, *Half and Half*, happens to have two opposing takes on being simultaneously Irish and Chinese. Claudine Chiawei O'Hearn, born in Hong Kong of an Irish American father and a Chinese mother, writes that 'My decision to study in Ireland on a semester abroad rather than in China, a country I have yet to visit, seemed to further confirm my predilection. I defended my choice because it conveniently fit my English major and why wouldn't I want to explore my Irish heritage. Truthfully, I was afraid to go to China because it was foreign to me.'[18] But Gish Jen writes: 'That my son, Luke, age four, goes to Chinese-culture school seems inevitable to most people, even though his father is of Irish descent. For certain ethnicities trump others; Chinese, for example trumps Irish. This has something to do with the relative distance of certain cultures from mainstream American culture, but it also has to do with race. For as we all know it is not certain ethnicities that trump others but certain colours; black trumps white, for example, always and forever; a mulatto is not a kind of white person, but a kind of black person.'[19] In Chiawei O'Hearn's description of her experience, being Irish allows her to escape, at least temporarily, from the harder option of being Chinese. In Jen's account, such an escape is essentially impossible because, when push comes to shove, Irish is white and white is part of the privileged mainstream.

But as Irish again becomes less white and more hybrid, we may find it useful to remember that globalisation is a part, not just of our present situation, but also of our own history. That history contains physical, social, sexual and imaginative connections with, among others, the Chinese. We have shared with them the hard work of creating some key moments of modernity and the experience of being victims of racist stereotypes. We have indulged in anti-Chinese racism and loved our Chinese husbands and children. Through our history, and in our ancestors as well as our own descendants, we know both the stupidity of racism and the richness of real human encounters – not as abstract principles but as real, lived experience.

.5.

Oscar Wilde's Chinese Sage

☆

JERUSHA McCORMACK

In February 1890, there appeared an extraordinary review. Under the title of 'A Chinese Sage', it hailed the 'first complete English translation' by Herbert A. Giles of the works of Zhuangzi (or Chuang Tsu, as he was then known under the older system of romanisation).[1] The author was Oscar Wilde.

The aftershock of this encounter is everywhere evident in Wilde's writing, the strongest evidence being a formidable list of parallel quotations, paraphrases and echoes of Zhuangzi, which is as startling as it is long.[2] But such a catalogue is only the beginning. No one who has ever read Zhuangzi and Wilde together at one sitting will miss the distinctive style which they both share: brilliant, unsettling and studded with epigrams which, as often as not, emerge as paradox or parody. Both Zhuangzi and Wilde resort to fables in order to illustrate complex intellectual stances. And both invent dazzling dialogues by which they turn entrenched social positions so completely inside out and upside down that eventually, as if by magic, they seem to be right side up.

Wilde did not necessarily learn these tricks from Zhuangzi. He probably adapted them, for the same reasons as Zhuangzi, as strategies by which to subvert a world which he had grown to oppose. In fact, Wilde's review of Zhuangzi occurred at the very moment when his own philosophy was beginning to take shape. It should not surprise us, then, that Zhuangzi's ideas become transformed into something cognate, yet quite distinct, within the writing of Oscar Wilde.

But surely there is something very odd about all of this. What indeed could have permitted an Irishman living in London in the late nineteenth century to be so receptive to a Chinese sage reputed to have lived in the fourth century BC? Along with Laozi (or Lao-Tsu, to whom is attributed the *Dao De Jing*), Zhuangzi is revered as one of the founders of the Daoist school of thought. The works translated by Giles probably circulated in something like their present form from the second century BC.[3] But what could have led Wilde to choose to respond so vividly to the thinking of a man who lived more than two thousand years ago in a land far away – and one separated by a virtual abyss in terms of civilisation?

In the broadest terms, both Zhuangzi and Wilde are what we might call 'contrarians'. This is a useful term for describing those who think against prevailing conventions in a way that appears to be systematically perverse, hence 'contrary' to the dominant discourse. Thus Wilde is often accused of merely inverting common epigrams in his own philosophical sayings, such as: 'Education is an admirable thing, but it is well to remember from time to time that nothing that is worth knowing can be taught.' Here is a sentiment derived directly from Zhuangzi, who tells the story of the wheelwright who, after many years as master of his craft, still can not teach his skills to his son.[4]

Contrarians are at their most useful during those times when conventions have been raised to ideals and when society is dominated by a consensus about these ideals. Thus Zhuangzi's main target was the literal overturning of Confucian sayings by stating them in terms of their opposite. Where Confucius preached the duty of right performance, Zhuangzi recommended doing nothing at all (the famous doctrine of *wu wei* or the 'principle of inaction' as it is sometimes translated), believing that man's perfection consisted in *being*, not in *doing*. In contrast to the instrumental morality of Confucius, Zhuangzi, with what Wilde identified as 'all the idealist's contempt for utilitarian systems', preached the uselessness of useful things. Thus Zhuangzi's campaign may be understood as not merely perverse, but a way of loosening what he must have seen as the stranglehold of Confucian thinking in his own age.

Similarly, Oscar Wilde arrived in England at a time when late Victorian society had reached a kind of claustrophobic consensus about the values and norms of their own 'proper' society. So over-whelming was this consensus that it was even personified as an elderly, judgmental (and ugly) woman called Mrs Grundy – dressed completely in black and often pictured with a furled umbrella, by which, it was implied, she would beat anyone who deviated from her own narrow standards.[5] Like Confucius, Mrs Grundy held to standards that were overwhelmingly moral, rather than aesthetic or philosophical. In fact, the kind of society advocated by Confucius and that of high Victorian England had many similarities. Both preached the supreme value of Duty within a rigid male hierarchy whose ideal was exemplified by the image of the 'gentleman'. Both believed in subordinating the individual to the group and art, as all other disciplines, to the service of morality. Thus one might risk the analogy that, as Confucius[6] was to Zhuangzi, so Mrs Grundy was to Oscar Wilde. Just as Zhuangzi baited the Confucian thinkers by inverting their dictates of right performance and duty, Wilde outraged the disciples of Mrs Grundy by turning their moral platitudes inside out, and thus making nonsense of them.[7]

Style was their agreed weapon. No one could ever be as serious as Confucius nor as oppressive as Mrs Grundy. So both Wilde and Zhuangzi resorted to the strategies of the frivolous. They told childish stories (Zhuangzi turned to fables; Wilde told stories as if for British children).[8] They both staged fake debates in which the odds were loaded on their side. Against the bare directives of authority, each evolved a distinctive style which was, in turn, playful, dazzling and subversive. By these means they reduced the logic of their opponents to chop-logic. When authorities spoke about the necessity of choice, these contrarians denied that choice was possible by arguing for the identity of opposites. If all else failed, they made their audiences laugh. That laugh is their battle-cry for, when oppressed by the *gravitas* of a collective moral rhetoric, laughter simply blows it up.

What Wilde discovered in Zhuangzi was a powerful ally. Wilde needed such an ally because, like Zhuangzi, he was an outsider. Whereas Zhuangzi was an outsider by choice, Wilde was one by birth. He was born into a country which had been England's first – and her oldest – colony. The Ireland of his birth was emerging from one of the most notorious famines on record, for which the Irish largely blamed the mismanagement of the English. Although Wilde at first seemed indifferent to his country of origin, about a year before he reviewed Zhuangzi he would describe himself as a 'most recalcitrant patriot'.[9] Nor could Wilde help observing in his review that 'were he [Zhuangzi] to come back to earth and visit us, he might have something to say to Mr Balfour about his coercion and active misgovernment in Ireland'.[10]

It is significant, too, that at the time his review of Zhuangzi was published – in February 1890 – Oscar Wilde was only beginning to make his popular mark as a writer. His novel *The Picture of Dorian Gray* was not to be published until the following June; the triumph of his first successful play, *Lady Windermere's Fan*, was still two years into the future. In fact, Wilde was regarded mostly as a talker and a socialite. It is a fact worth noting that everything that Wilde wrote (and is famous for writing) appears *after* his reading/reviewing of Zhuangzi. Of course, given the breadth of Wilde's reading and the multitude of his sources, it would be foolish to say that any one author could account as a determining influence.[11] But from the available evidence, it is clear that the discovery of Zhuangzi was a crucial agent in transforming Wilde into the notorious wit, writer and, above all, the brilliant thinker that we recognise today.[12]

To make this point, one only has to look at the two works written shortly after his review to see how Zhuangzi helped Wilde to formulate some of his most revolutionary ideas. Wilde's famous essay 'The Soul of Man under Socialism' was published in the *Fortnightly Review* in February 1891 – exactly a year after the piece on Zhuangzi. It is the only Wilde essay that is usually read 'straight', that is, as sincere and from the heart. But it soon dawns on an attentive reader that what is being advocated here is not socialism at all but (in the terms of Western politics) pure anarchy. For here Wilde argues for nothing less than the abolition of all authority, since 'all authority is quite degrading. It degrades those who exercise it, and degrades those over whom it is exercised.'[13]

Although the Chinese thinker has been described by one expert as 'perhaps the world's first anarchist', it would be unjustified to ascribe such an extreme sentiment only to Wilde's reading of Zhuangzi,[14] What Zhuangzi's text provided was a catalyst – in the sense that he helped to crystallise Wilde's thought into something clearly radical. What Wilde discovered in Zhuangzi was, as he states in the very first sentence of his review, nothing less than 'the most caustic criticism of modern life I have met with for some time ... Chuang Tsu [Wilde continues] ... sought to destroy society, as we know it, as the middle classes know it.' If the ordinary citizen 'really knew who he was, they would tremble', Wilde adds: for Zhuangzi's thinking is, in fact, 'excessively dangerous'.[15]

It is a thinking Wilde himself sought to emulate. From its first notorious sentence, 'The Soul of Man under Socialism' resonates with echoes of the Chinese sage. Boldly paraphrasing Zhuangzi, Wilde focuses on those bastions of Victorian middle-class society, the do-gooders, by showing how 'They try to solve the problem of poverty ... by keeping the poor alive; or, in the case of a very advanced school, by amusing the poor.' Yet poverty itself, Wilde argues, would no longer exist if it were not kept in place by such well-intentioned philanthropy. In sustaining existing conditions rather than changing them, Wilde insists, the work of such do-gooders both degrades and demoralises. In short, he concludes, 'Charity creates a multitude of sins.'[16]

It is no accident that the philanthropists excoriated by Wilde have much in common with the do-gooders of Zhuangzi. But Zhuangzi would not have been his only source. Wilde would have found much the same rhetoric in passages from the Stoics – or from the Gospels. For Jesus of Nazareth did teach many of the same things as Zhuangzi: that a man's real riches were internal, that he should give away his property in order to become perfected and that man's spiritual needs were greater than his material ones.

At the same time, reading the life of Jesus through the lens of Zhuangzi gave Wilde a radically new perspective. For example, in his prose-poem 'The Doer of Good', Wilde depicts Jesus meeting, one by one, the people whose lives he had once transformed. The leper he had cured is now a drunk. When asked by Jesus, 'Why do you live like this?' he replied: 'I was a leper, and you healed me. How else should I live?' The blind man he made see has taken up with prostitutes. When asked why, he replies: 'I was blind and you gave me sight. At what else should I look?' Proceeding further into the city, Jesus recognises a familiar figure. Running forward, he detains her, asking: 'Is there no other way in which to walk save the way of sin?'

> And the woman turned round and recognised Him, and laughed and said, 'But you forgave me my sins, and the way is a pleasant way.'

> And He [Jesus] passed out of the city.

> And when He had passed out of the city He saw seated by the roadside a young man who was weeping.

> And He went towards him and touched the long locks of his hair and said to him, 'Why are you weeping?'

And the young man looked up and recognised Him and made answer, 'But I was dead once and you raised me from the dead. What else should I do but weep?'[17]

Yeats called this 'the best short story in the world', precisely because it violently inverted sacred Christian values.[18]

Thus, as Zhuangzi predicted, the effects of doing good do not turn out, in fact, to be 'good'. As Zhuangzi saw it, interference with the system – disguised as virtue – in fact becomes the means of keeping the system going. And for Wilde, as for Zhuangzi, the greatest interference is done in the name of government. In 'The Soul of Man under Socialism', Wilde states Zhuangzi's position at its most succinct: 'All modes of government are failures.'[19] Here Wilde declares war not merely on established government, but on all authority whatsoever, claiming that in life

> There are three kinds of despots … The first is called the Prince. The second is called the Pope … The third is called the People.[20]

Although he does not name his source, Wilde's manifesto clearly echoes Zhuangzi's stark dismissal of the same trio of public authorities – invoking even the same semantic triad:

> 'There is the sword of the Son of Heaven,' said Chuang Tsu, 'the sword of the Princes, and the sword of the People.'[21]

Of these three, the 'sword of the People' is regarded as especially dangerous because, unlike official authority, it enforces convention as if it were an ideal worth following. In referring to this danger, Wilde remarked in his review that, 'as for a thoroughly sympathetic man, he is, in the eyes of Chuang Tsu, simply a man who is always trying to be somebody else, and so misses the only possible excuse for his existence'.[22]

Thus, above all, what Zhuangzi's teaching helped to clarify in Wilde's mind was the necessity of escaping social conformity. As he observes in 'The Soul of Man under Socialism', 'People … go through their lives … without ever realising that they are probably thinking other people's thoughts, living by other people's standards, wearing practically what one may call other people's second-hand clothes, and never being themselves for a single moment.' Then, quoting Zhuangzi but without identifying him, Wilde continues: '"He who would be free," says a fine thinker, "must not conform." And authority, by bribing people to conform, produces a very gross kind of over-fed barbarism amongst us.'[23]

It is in these terms that Wilde appropriates Zhuangzi's rhetoric of self-realisation – but for his own ends. Wilde's arguments are formulated most crucially in the two parts of his famous essay called 'The Critic as Artist', published just months after his review of Zhuangzi.[24]

In fact, Zhuangzi's whole philosophy of inaction might be summed up in the subtitle to Part I of 'The Critic as Artist: With some Remarks upon the Importance of Doing Nothing.' Compare this with Zhuangzi: '[The sage's] virtue should be passive, not active. He should *be* rather than *do*.'[25] But whereas Zhuangzi's philosophy of *wu wei* carefully balances action and contemplation, Wilde comes down roundly on the side of inaction. Thus he has his spokesman Gilbert state that 'It is very much more difficult to talk about a thing than to do it,' and 'to do nothing at all is the most difficult thing in the world, the most difficult and the most intellectual.' Moreover, this inaction becomes the very premise of personal development, as 'the contemplative life, [is] the life that has for its aim not *doing*, but *being*, and not *being* merely, but *becoming* …'.[26]

To aim to *be* rather than to *do* is to move from a moral into a purely aesthetic world. By invoking Zhuangzi's advocacy of *wu wei* (or the 'principle of inaction'), Wilde hit on a method by which each man could become potentially not merely an artist, but the artist of his own life. In short, Zhuangzi helped provide Wilde with the formulae that were to form the basis of his unique philosophy of dandyism.

Although today we may think of a dandy as a man of fashion, or even as a man obsessed with style, for Wilde and his contemporaries the dandy was the spiritual epitome of his civilisation.[27] In the dandy, all the virtues of his culture were embodied: he was the Victorian gentleman liberated from the prison-house of morality, that is, from the confines of public conformity – just as, for Zhuangzi, the perfected man was a man liberated from the bondage of Confucian dictates.

In these accounts, it is important to note that this perfected being was, for both Wilde and Zhuangzi, a man; that is, male. And not merely a man, but a man of leisure. In 'The Soul of Man under Socialism' Wilde posited an ideal society in which every person might enjoy the dandy's privileges of leisure, freedom and culture. In common with others of his time, Wilde understood that anarchism, far from being democracy carried to its logical end, is much nearer to an aristocracy universalised and purified: that is, not an order of free noblemen but one of noble and free men.[28] Likewise Zhuangzi preached a way of living in which a person, freed from duties towards family, other citizens and the state, could devote himself to the self-culture normally reserved for the mandarin. In fact, as he is depicted, Zhuangzi was a thorn in the side of those officials who saw his intelligence but could not get him to commit himself to government service: a highway to prestige in that world, yet one which Zhuangzi despised. For, although poor, Zhuangzi regarded himself as already living as an aristocrat, insofar as he had absolute sovereignty over his own life.

Ultimately Wilde and Zhuangzi both made their lives outside the prevailing moral dictates of their time but saw their stance in very different ways. For Zhuangzi, to do so asserted a spiritual freedom. For Wilde, this spiritual freedom was expressed as a form of power. His dandy/gentlemen use this power to rescue others from the moral formulae by which they have become entrapped in destructive scenarios. By detaching them from 'moral' plati-tudes in the name of a contemplative or aesthetic perspective, the dandy shows them the route to escape. Accordingly, the dandy masters others by persuading them of the importance of style over substance, or of manners over morals.[29] In his disdain for the merely moral concerns of the world, Wilde's dandy achieves a kind of freedom.

Thus, in the end, reading Zhuangzi appears to have given Wilde the confidence to live, as well as to write, as a contrarian. If Wilde's life came to a disastrous end, his writing has, like Zhuangzi's, transformed the world in which he lived. And that writing is everywhere suffused not only with the doctrines of the Chinese sage but by his singularly contrarian style. As one example, consider a famous story by Zhuangzi, telling how

> Once upon a time, I, Chuang Tsu, dreamt I was a butterfly, fluttering hither and thither, to all intents and purposes a butterfly … Suddenly I awaked, and there I lay, myself again. Now I do not know whether I was then a man dreaming I was a butterfly, or whether I am now a butterfly dreaming I am a man.[30]

As Zhuangzi well knew, moral discourse is founded on a consensus of what is 'real'. But what is 'real' is upended in this discourse forever. In the world of Zhuangzi's butterfly no moral choice is possible, only sustained contemplation of the shifting nature of 'reality'. In a very similar manoeuvre in his essay 'The Decay of Lying', Wilde overturns the Western truism that Art imitates Nature and, with it, all of previous Western aesthetics. Not only does he overturn it, but he does so deftly and wittily. Wilde's style is so light-hearted that it has taken a long time for him to be regarded as a serious thinker. In fact, Wilde and Zhuangzi are the only philosophers I can think of who display a sense of humour. It leads one to wonder if perhaps the most important thing that Wilde learned from Zhuangzi is that even a serious thinker can be mischievous – and that making people laugh is an effective way of opening them up to new intellectual positions.

One might go even further. By showing in 'The Decay of Lying' how our actual perception of Nature is determined by the images of Art, Wilde also lays the foundation for the thinking that ushers in the modern West, whether one is considering the revolution of *gestalt* psychology or post-modern views of the nature of reality and selfhood. If one understands Wilde's essays in this light, one can see why such a figure as Thomas Mann already found in the writing of Oscar Wilde much of the revolutionary philosophy of Friedrich Nietzsche, his 'furious war against morality' and his transvaluation of moral into aesthetic values.[31] Wilde had not read Nietzsche. Nor did he need him. He had already found validation for his own revolutionary thinking formulated in the writings of a fellow-spirit who lived more than two thousand years earlier in a distant and, to many, incomprehensible civilisation, that of China. And, together in spirit with Zhuangzi, Oscar Wilde set about changing forever the course of intellectual work, particularly that of aesthetics, not only in his Britain, not only in Europe, but in the entire Western world.

It is a suitable irony that his essay on 'The Soul of Man under Socialism' became, after Wilde's death, a favourite among the champions of the Young China movement,[32] for it is one of the best examples of how traditional Chinese thinking has not only changed other worlds but has come home to inspire, once again, the civilisation in which it was born.

.6.

Transplanting China to Ireland:

Three Generations of the Earls of Rosse

BRENDAN PARSONS, *Seventh Earl of Rosse*

Most people who have heard of Birr, in the very heart of Ireland, think of it as the place of that great monster telescope, which could see furthest into space up to the second decade of the twentieth century. That was built by my great-great-grandfather, William Parsons, the 3rd Earl, in the 1840s. It is now to be admired by all, restored, in the centre of the castle's park, or 'Demesne' (to use the old Norman word), covering within a great encircling wall all the garden area of more than fifty hectares. **[figure 11]**

Others, maybe more in the know, see Birr Castle as the home which produced William's youngest son, Charles Parsons. It was Charles who invented a steam turbine which propelled ships faster than ever before and quite revolutionised marine transport as a result.

Others still know Birr as one of the great gardens of Europe; indeed the only one in Ireland to figure in the latest book on its thirty, supposedly, top gardens. Few people, however, seem to have wondered where most of its thousands of plants have actually come from, who collected them and how they happen to be thriving so well. Here in Birr these plants are setting many records, as well as inspiring an increasing number of artists to paint them in all their beauty.

The resulting paintings have been assembled for a series of exhibitions specially entitled *Flora Birrensis*. Those who have come to see these exhibitions have been struck by many things, including the surprising fact that, of all the plants painted from all over the world at Birr, far more come from China than from anywhere else, since over 40 per cent of the total are of Chinese origin. This same dominance of Chinese plants at Birr is to be noted in two other publications. The first of these is the Tree Register's *Champion Trees of Britain and Ireland*, crediting Birr with the greatest number of champion trees in Ireland. No less than sixteen of these come from China. Finally, in the demesne's own booklet, its *Red Tree Trail of Fifty Trees of Distinction*, no less than one-quarter of the total come from China. Plants at Birr have come from perhaps as many as forty different countries (I myself have collected seed in as many as sixteen different countries) and provenance ranges very much from the Northern to the Southern hemispheres. All the same, those from China far, far outnumber those from any other country, including the United States.

Although so much of Birr's most important and beautiful flora thus comes from China, in general, it is interesting to find Birr Castle's archives and botanical library showing that most in fact originate from one region. This is the area stretching from the centre to the southwest of China, and in particular from the provinces of Szechuan (Sichuan) and especially Yunnan. Surely their success at Birr must have something to do with the rainfall in our region, which averages only a fraction over 100 centimetres a year – closer to that of the valleys of Yunnan, at the fringe of the monsoon area, than to more central parts of China, which would have less regular precipitation and far greater extremes of temperature. In spite of the soil in Birr being less acidic than that in Yunnan, many of the supposedly lime-hating plants such as Magnolias, and even some Rhododendrons, succeed well enough at Birr to be greatly admired.

The story of the introduction of the first Chinese plants at Birr goes back just over a century from now, to another Irishman, Augustine Henry. Henry came from an old Irish family called Ollnnevigh, which was from what is now Northern Ireland, and being Catholic, lost most of its lands during the establishment of Protestant settlers several centuries before. Brought up to a very simple life, he managed to get a place at the new Queen's College in Galway, where he earned a gold medal and first-class honours. These took him to Queen's University, Belfast, where, in turn, he received a degree in Medicine in 1879. As that was the qualification then being sought by the Imperial Chinese Customs Service, he was duly recruited. When he went out to join that service in 1881, he was promptly sent the thousand kilometres up the Yangtze River to Ichang (Yichang, Hubei province). It is just to the west of there, where the Yangtze breaks out of the mountains, that many of the best plants now at Birr came to be found, and we are fortunate indeed that Henry was based there for more than a decade with much time and energy to explore.

His discoveries to the west of Ichang are best reflected in the many plants which are now scientifically named after him. To name only a few, these include *Emenopterys henryana, Rhododendron augustinii, Tilia henryana*. Of these three, many specimens can now be admired in the gardens of Birr, and the last two were specially painted for publication in respectively *Flora Birrensis* and *A Prospect of Irish Flowers*.

Many of the most important plants now at Birr go back to my grandfather's correspondence with Augustine Henry, beginning as soon as he inherited Birr in 1908. By this time, Henry's explorations into cataloguing unknown Chinese flora were formidable. As we now know, the plants actually named after Henry in fact comprise only a very small proportion of the hundreds which he is credited with discovering. He started collecting and sending specimens of the seeds back to the Royal Botanic Gardens in Kew for identification in 1885. These include some of the most beautiful trees ever found, such as the famous 'dove' or 'handkerchief' tree *Davidia involucrata*; the most sweetly scented and spectacular *Magnolia officinalis*, or Incense Magnolia (here illustrated with a painting by Patricia Jorgensen; see **figure 12**); the graceful *Itea ilicifolia*, to be found today in Birr's secret winter garden; the *Hamamellis mollis*; the rare Chinese rubber tree *Eucommia ulmoides*, of which we have specimens in two places at Birr; or the equally rare *Decumaria sinensis* which literally covers the face of Birr Castle right up to the battlements on the roof. All these great flowering wonders from China can now be admired at Birr thanks to Augustine Henry, or the 'scholarly Irishman' as he was called by fellow Europeans in China. As to how the Chinese scholars themselves saw him, we can do no better than to refer to the second collection of the *Icones Plantarium Sinicarium* published by Academia Sinica (or the Chinese Academy of Sciences), which was actually dedicated to Augustine Henry. A copy presented to my own father by T.T.Yu (of whom we shall learn more) gives the dedication in these words:

> To Augustine Henry, through whose assiduous botanical exploration of Central and South-Western China, the knowledge of our flora has been greatly extended.

My grandfather did not limit his correspondence to Augustine Henry. Keen to experiment with all sorts of plants being recently discovered in China, he also subscribed to other plant-hunting expeditions as well as ordering plants directly from suppliers both in France and in London. Thus he procured, just before the outbreak of World War One in 1914, and for the sums of thirteen old French francs and six English shillings respectively, the two following plants which figure as probably the greatest stars on our *Red Tree Trail*:

China *and the* Irish

The huge *Magnolia delavayi* on the castle terrace against the wall of the castle's moat; and

the rare *Carrierea calycina* which features in the 2007 December issue of the *The Plantsman* magazine.

The last must be the finest of all the many rare Chinese trees to be found at Birr. We had to wait eighty years to see it flower for the first time – but then, so luminous did it appear, we could admire its beauty even by moonlight.

In our family history, it is my uncle Desmond who provides the most vivid relationship with China. Desmond Parsons was the aesthetic younger brother of my father Michael. Never really happy in either Britain or Ireland, but a good natural linguist with fluency in both French and German, he travelled extensively round Europe before moving out to China.

On arrival in Peking (modern Beijing), Desmond promptly started both learning Chinese and teaching languages in the university. He set up house in *hutong Tsin Hua* number 8, which he entirely furnished in the most perfect traditional Chinese style. It was here that he started collecting not just Chinese porcelain, fans, screens and robes, but particularly the most beautiful Chinese scrolls, which are still preserved in chests at Birr. It was here that Desmond translated his first book, on Chinese folk or fairy tales, and here that he entertained guests along with the fellow aesthete who had come to join him in Peking, Harold Acton. **[figure 13]** It was also in this *hutong* that Desmond built up a circle of both European and Chinese friends who proved of singular importance when my parents came out for a very extended stopover on their honeymoon in 1935.

While his brother was establishing himself in Peking, my father, Michael, continued the tradition established by his own father: subscribing first to more plant-hunting expeditions, such as those of Kingdon-Ward to the area around Eastern Tibet. He then actually went to Tibet himself, while still a bachelor, even if decidedly uncomfortable both riding a yak and drinking Tibetan tea. Then, after my parents married, they came out to

China on their honeymoon and met Desmond's circle of friends in Peking.

One of these was Prince Pu Ru, a cousin of the last emperor and once considered as an heir, by then a humble painter who gave and dedicated personally to my mother quite a simple small fan, which we have carefully preserved as part of our most cherished heritage at Birr.

Another friend was the director of Peking's Fan Institute of Biology, Professor H.H. Hu. It was with Professor Hu that my father then arranged for the three key plant-hunting expeditions, to be led by T.T.Yu. Extending over the period of 1937–39, these expeditions produced the seed for other Chinese champion trees to be found now at Birr, such as the *Tilia henryana*. Even more notably, my father's botanical correspondence at Birr also reveals one of the earliest descriptions of the discovery of the fossil tree, *Metasequoia glyptostroboides*, in Szechuan. It also records that my father was noted as 'the first European friend' to whom my uncle Desmond's friend, Professor H.H. Hu, sent the seed in January 1948. Alas that seed never germinated, but the next one seems to have done so later that year, thereby producing the first planting of *Metasequoia glyptostroboides* in Ireland, in 1951 – still of course to be admired at Birr today.

Very sadly the *hutong* in which my uncle Desmond once lived stands no more today, having fallen, along with many of Beijing's one-storey traditional dwellings, in the path of developers. Sadly too, Desmond himself did not long survive the valuable introductions he effected there. His dream had long been somehow to get to the early Buddhist caves of Dunhuang (in Shazhou, Gansu provice, located in the far northwest of China) in order to record the paintings on their walls with the camera, which was his favourite tool. These Mogao caves are now a World Heritage site of UNESCO and one which, three years ago now, we were able to admire ourselves at the end of a comfortable bus tour along the old Silk Road. Over seventy years earlier, however, travel there was dangerous enough for Desmond's return to prove ultimately fatal for him. After five full days producing, ironically with the help of a local policeman, the photographic record of the caves (now in the custody of the School of Oriental and Asian Studies at the University of London), Desmond embarked on the long return journey, only to be arrested and incarcerated in a prison cell. Though relatively speedily released, after British diplomatic pressure, Desmond eventually got back to Peking literally a dying man: doctors diagnosed him as then suffering from not just one incurable disease, but two. My parents brought him back to Europe on the trans-Siberian railway over the New Year of 1936, but he eventually expired a year later in a sanatorium in Switzerland.

By the time I myself followed in my parents' footsteps to Yunnan in 1993, our elder son, Patrick, was studying at the Beijing Language Institute. When Patrick had decided he wanted to go to China, he started in Hong Kong but very soon realised that that was not the 'real China'. He sent back almost a one-liner asking if we would support his going up to Beijing to learn Chinese properly at its famous language institute there. Nothing has given us greater pleasure than doing this, particularly when we found that by the end of his first year there, Patrick was already supporting himself by getting small parts in a film series, in which he was cast, I might say, as a 'foreign devil'. Although he was, for a year or two after this, occasionally shunned on the streets of Beijing, his excursion into film-making does not seem to have adversely affected his subsequent career in the Chinese real-estate market, which he has been pursuing for now well over a full decade.

Patrick started off managing the research department of the estate agents Jones Lang Wootton. Since then he has intentionally, and I think most unusually for a European, worked on purely Chinese developments: most recently for the Yinan group, of which he is currently acting as executive president. Here he is responsible for twelve projects, including two islands and a mountain resort as well as central city sites being developed in Hebei, Fujian and Liaoning Provinces. Patrick has also helped set up an Irish Investment Consulting company, IIA, of which he serves as strategic partner and director.

Just in case the above has not been enough to keep him busy professionally, Patrick has also served for the three years as

Chairman of the Irish Network China (INC). This period was of exceptional importance, as it included the first Irish state visit to China as well as the strongest government and trade missions Ireland had yet fielded. Finally, then, Patrick was appointed Ireland's Olympic Attaché for what was of course to become, last year in Beijing, the greatest Olympic Games the world has yet seen!

There is still far more to say about our elder son Patrick, for he has also married into China. His wife is a talented television presenter from Tientsin, Anna Lin. During their traditional Chinese wedding ceremony in Beijing, passers-by and drivers of vehicles were brought to a standstill at the spectacle of the palanquin carrying the bride to become my daughter-in-law. The actual wedding ceremony in China was then followed by a ceremony of Christian blessing back in Ireland. Since then, Anna has already given us our first grandchildren. First came Olivia Rose Xuewei, because she appeared in January, like a winter rose; indeed not only that, but on the date of 8 January, whose good luck even we have now become Chinese enough to appreciate as well! Now already aged three, and naturally bilingual, she has now been joined by a young brother, William Charles Yufan; so we find ourselves the grandparents of two sino-hibernian infants, as we proudly see them, like the peonies in the garden at Birr.

Our second son, Michael, twelve years Patrick's junior, is different in many ways. Whether by example, a sense of tradition or straight inspiration, Michael has also felt drawn to China. Following Patrick's footsteps, he has learnt as much Chinese as he could quickly at the Beijing International Studies University and then started teaching English both at Xidan primary school and at Bai Nian Vocational School, which provides free education and training for the children of migrant workers in Beijing. As a new school starting in a new field with an inadequate budget, it needed everything, from a special curriculum to teaching materials and equipment. In response to this need, Michael got his friends and family to support a fund-raising overland trip to Tibet, which raised a surplus of 24,000 RMB – enough to equip and sustain the English language teaching at the school for the next year. In September 2006, Michael then joined Beijing's Education Forum for Asia, first as Project Officer, then as Communications Manager. As such he helped arrange and support the forum's annual conferences for both 2006 and 2007 as well as the Yanji International Tourism Conference. Most recently, in 2008, he has spent his last six months in China as an intern with the Press and Information Section at the Delegation of the European Commission in Beijing.

If our only daughter Alicia is more Persian than Chinese, this is only to be expected, since she was born and first brought up when I was based in Iran with the United Nations Development Programme. She has also been out to China, most recently as a surprise for my seventieth birthday, which Patrick arranged for me to celebrate in almost imperial style overlooking the Forbidden City in Beijing. However when she herself married a fellow Irishman in Dublin the year before last, she carried up the aisle to her wedding, instead of a bouquet, just one single flower: that was not just a Chinese Magnolia but the loveliest and most sweetly scented one discovered by Augustine Henry: *Magnolia officinalis*, most aptly known as 'the Incense Magnolia'. Destiny had brought this specially into flower at Birr just in time to adorn and bless Alicia with its singular beauty, in perfect harmony with the actual incense used for the wedding service itself.

Having sought to focus on our own extensive family links with China – as well as the richness of the Chinese flora they have introduced to Birr – I would like to end by sharing with you a no less interesting record, I believe, of those from China who have managed to make it to Birr.

The very first party that visited Birr, when I took over after the death of my father, was the Chinese olympic archery team led by Li Tianmin. This team spent two days at Birr in May 1980, shooting at targets straight in front of the castle and never missing (there was some anxiety about arrows flying through our windows!). Who could have then imagined that that very castle, where that Chinese olympic team was then competing, would eventually provide Ireland's Olympic Attaché for the first Olympic Games to be staged in Beijing some twenty-eight years later?

Meanwhile, in 1982, Birr was honoured by the visit of China's first full ambassador, Mme Gong Pusheng, to whom we were then able to present a bouquet of our very own cross of Chinese peonies raised in Birr, named 'Anne Rosse'. **[figure 14]** Her visit to see the beautiful flowers of China thriving at Birr has since been followed by two further Chinese ambassadors: Dr Sha Hailin, in 2005, and his successor, Ambassador Zhang Xinsen, the year before last.

In 1986, three key officials of the Beijing Botanic Gardens and the Institutes of Botany in both Beijing and Guangzhou (Canton) spent two days at Birr with Dr E.C. Nelson of the Botanic Gardens, Glasnevin, laying the foundations for real botanic coop-eration. This eventually led to pairs of skilled botanical technicians being flown out from China for assignments at Birr under the auspices of the China Association for International Exchange of Personnel. Two each came from the botanical institutes and gardens in Beijing and Kunming (capital of Yunnan province). These young botanical technicians clarified the identification of many plants from China and compiled books of specimens for a herbarium. We have had, over the years, many dozens of interns from around the world, but we believe about the best work ever done was by Tang Yu Dan, who has left behind the record of her work in the form of books identifying, for instance, our collection of oak trees at Birr. There is room for much more such work at Birr, to study how the growth of Chinese plants here may compare with that of plants back in China.

I myself have no formal qualification as a botanist, horticul-turalist, forester, landscape architect or anything else to qualify me other than the degree in history and training in development economics on which I have based my own career in the service of the UN in both Africa and Asia. But, looking back, what has fascinated me has been to note that most of the plants which seem to be the greatest success in Birr also come from the same country as that which both increasingly draws our family to it and looks likely to become our fastest-growing market for tourism. Two or three years ago, Birr was unknown as a tourist destination for Chinese tour groups. Yet, last year, Birr received seven times more Chinese groups on a commercial basis than the year before, including a group of principals of key schools in Shanghai, thus opening up the spectrum of educational tourism. We have therefore already started to make our basic tourist information available in Chinese.

Over the last century, our family's history has literally been implanted in the garden at Birr. Our special interest in China is everywhere there, from the star plants to the champion trees. We believe we have more unique and sustained links with China than anywhere else in Ireland, except perhaps those of the Chester Beatty Library in Dublin Castle. These are the connections that make us look forward to a future when we may welcome as many Chinese visitors to Birr as we now do Americans and fellow Europeans – hoping that they will, in this small but precious demesne, discover how successfully China can be not only transplanted into Ireland but also now thrive there in our own native soil.

Figure 1: *The Qianlong Emperor in Ceremonial Armour on Horseback* by Giuseppe Castiglione (Ch. Lang Shining; 1688–1766) 1739 or 1758. Hanging scroll (originally a *tieluo* painting); ink and colour on silk, 322.5 x 232 cm. © The Palace Museum, Beijing.

Figure 2: *The Relief of the Black River Camp* from the series *Quelling the Rebellion in the Western Regions*. Copper-plate engraving, based on a drawing by Giuseppe Castiglione, by Le Bas, 1771. © Trustees of the Chester Beatty Library.

Figure 3: *The Emperor of China Receiving the Ambassador at Jehol, Tartary* by William Alexander (1767–1816). Pencil, pen-and-ink, wash and watercolour, from the *Album of 278 Drawings of Landscapes, Coastlines, Costumes and Everyday Life Made During Lord Macartney's Embassy to the Emperor of China*. Originally produced 1792–94. © All Rights Reserved. The British Library Board. Licence no. THECHE 01.

Figure 4: *Reception of the Diplomatique and his Suite at the Court of Pekin,*
c.1793 (colour etching) by James Gillray.
Courtesy of the Victoria & Albert Museum, London, UK/ The Bridgeman Art Library.

Figure 5: Sir Robert Hart and family: his wife Hester Jane Bredon (Hessie) with their two children Evelyn Amy (Evey) and Edgar Bruce in 1878. A third daughter, Mabel Milburne (Nollie) was born later. © Queen's University Belfast, Sir Robert Hart Collection, MS 15.

Figure 6: 'Man of the Day', *Vanity Fair* (No. 608, 27 December 1894).
This cartoon clearly comments on what the British audience saw as
Robert Hart's rather suspect hybrid identity in his role as an agent for
both British and Chinese interests. © Queen's University Belfast,
Sir Robert Hart Collection, MS 15.

Figure 7: Promontory Point, Utah (1869).
Despite being among the 'cosmopolitan' crowd celebrating the completion of the transcontinental railroad
on 10 May 1869, Chinese railroad workers were deliberately excluded from the official photographs.

Figure 8: Ticket for the Workingmen's Party of California founded by the Cork-born Labour leader,
Denis Kearney. Dated as 1879, the original lithograph is by the artist Carl Albert Browne.
© California Historical Society, FN.

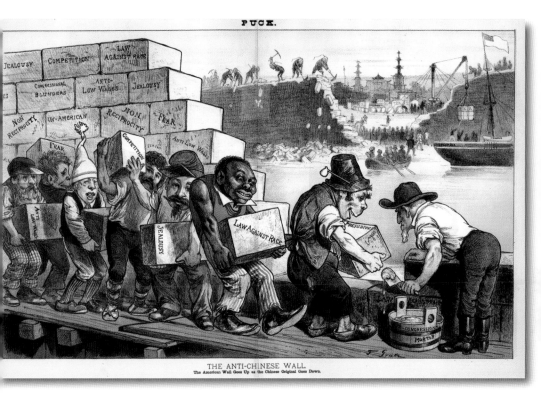

Figure 9: The Anti-Chinese Wall ('The American Wall Goes Up as the Chinese Original Comes Down') *Puck* (*c.* 1880). Note the new solidarity of the Irish with other non-Chinese immigrant groups (including those from Europe) as the first in line to oust the Chinese. Courtesy of Michigan State University Museum.

Figure 10: Cover of *Yankee Notions* (March 1858) entitled 'The Result of the Immigration from China'. The caption reads:

Mrs Chang-Fee-Chow-Cry *(the better half of the Celestial over the way):*
'..., Chang-Mike, run home and take Pat-Chow and Rooney-Sing wid ye, and bring the last of the ... pie for yer daddy. And, do ye mind? bring some praties for yer mother, ye spalpeens.'
(To her husband) 'How be's ye, Chang-Honey?'
Chang-Honey 'Sky wi po kee bang too, mucho puck ti, rum foo, toodle skee sicks!'

.7.

'Heroism and Zeal':

Pioneers of the Irish Christian Missions to China

PATRICK COMERFORD
and RICHARD O'LEARY

'In the past most of the priests Ireland could spare were sent to America and Australia, to minister to our exiled people, but now conditions in these countries are rapidly changing. Many of the American and Australian dioceses are self-supporting, and Ireland is comparatively free to turn her attention to the heathen world. What glorious conquests await her!'[1] So wrote a young Irish Catholic priest in China, Fr Edward Galvin, in a letter to student priests in Ireland in 1915. Galvin was one of a number of Irish Christians, Catholic and Protestant, who may be regarded as pioneers of the Irish missions to China. This essay recalls these

Irish missionaries and records something of the impact they had both on Ireland and on China.

Christianity was first brought to China by Nestorian Christians in the seventh century. Of Christian missionaries, the Roman Catholics were the earliest to arrive in China. What began with a small number of Jesuits in the sixteenth century grew into the more substantial missionary endeavours in the nineteenth and twentieth centuries, especially the French. However, overall Christians were numerically a tiny religious group in pre-Communist China.

The first Protestant missionary to China was Robert Morrison from the London Missionary Society, who arrived in Macao in 1807. But the first Anglican missionaries did not arrive in China until the 1840s. Among them were three graduates of Trinity College, Dublin, including William Armstrong Russell, who was to become the first Irish bishop in China. Russell and three other Protestant bishops from the Church of Ireland were to become key figures in the formation of an independent indigenous Anglican Church in China.

The first Irish Catholic Mission to China came much later, with the Missionary Society of Saint Columban.[2] Popularly known as the Maynooth Mission to China, this was co-founded in 1916 by Fr Edward Galvin who was later to become Bishop of Hanyang (now a district in Wuhan, Hubei province in central China). **[Figure 15]** Galvin, his co-founder Fr John Blowick and Lady Moloney (who founded the Columban Sisters) were missionary pioneers, who, aside from their work in China, created a major new indigenous Irish Catholic organisation for the foreign missions. In doing so they greatly raised awareness among the general population in Ireland about both the foreign missionary endeavour and about China.

Edward Galvin (1882–1956) from Newcestown, County Cork, was ordained a Catholic priest at St Patrick's College, Maynooth, in 1909. Although intended to serve in his home diocese of Cork, he spent the next three years as a priest on loan to the diocese of Brooklyn, New York. Already convinced he wished to be a missionary, Galvin read every book that he could find about China in the Brooklyn public library. It was at this point that he met a Canadian missionary priest. Fr Fraser was about to return to China after lecturing in Ireland and in the United States about the missions; it was he who persuaded Galvin to leave with him.

During his first years in China, between 1912 and 1916, Fr Galvin lived and worked with French Vincentian missionaries in Zhejiang province. But he kept in touch with Ireland, writing letters not just to his family at home but also to students and priests at the national seminary at Maynooth, exhorting them to commit to work in China.[3] As he wrote to one student at Maynooth: 'I hope to see the day when Ireland will be fully equipped for the missions, when she will have a national missionary college, as France has, as Belgium has, as America has, whose influence will reach out to every part of the country and gather in men, who will give up all for God and souls.'[4]

Fr Galvin believed that the Catholic Church in Ireland was now sufficiently strong to rise to the challenge of a China mission; he advised seminarians at Maynooth accordingly (see opening quotation). In mid-1914 he received word that two of his correspondents, Joseph O'Leary of Cork and Patrick O'Reilly of Cavan, had committed their lives to China and were coming to join him within the year. At the time, the Catholic mission field was dominated by French missionaries who, the Irish priests felt, had somewhat different methods and ideals from their own. Fathers Galvin and O'Leary believed that the contribution from Ireland to the missions in China would be enhanced if Ireland had its own Irish China missionary society. 'I wonder will Irish secular priests ever have an Irish Vicarate here,' Fr O'Leary wrote from China. 'There is plenty of room for one in China. I believe if they could get one, they would be the most successful missionaries that ever came here. The French are splendid of course, but they are very conservative. They are gentlemen to their finger tips but they will almost legislate on a man's soutane or the number of hairs in his beard.'[5]

Once in China, these three priests – Frs Galvin, O'Leary and O'Reilly – mapped out what was required: an Irish foreign missionary society for China, with its own seminary in Ireland; an Irish Vicarate in China approved by Rome as missionary territory where the Irish missionaries would work together; and the support of the Irish diaspora.[6] With these objectives in mind, Fr Galvin returned to Ireland in 1916.

Fr Galvin was aware that, as a young and relatively junior priest, he would need to find more powerful figures in the Catholic Church in Ireland who could advance his project. With this in mind, he decided to approach Fr John Blowick. Born in 1888 in Belcarra, Co. Mayo, by 1916 John Blowick was Professor of Dogmatic Theology at St Patrick's College, Maynooth. Stirred by Fr Fraser's enthusiasm for the missions in China, Blowick agreed to bring a proposal to the meeting of the Irish bishops at Maynooth in October 1916 outlining their joint proposal for a new Irish mission to China. The outcome exceeded expectations. Going far beyond minimal approval for the new St Columban's Foreign Mission Society, the bishops issued a public statement that they 'joyfully approve and bless the project and earnestly commend to the generous help and support of the faithful the establishment of this Mission House for the training of Irish missionaries for China, who, in a spirit worthy of our missionary race, offer their lives for the propagation of the Faith in a pagan country'.[7]

The new society was to be called after St Columbanus, a famous Irish-born missionary from the sixth century, a time when Irish Christian monks were renowned for their foreign missions to largely pagan Western Europe. By virtue of such naming, the Foreign Mission Society hoped to recapture some of Ireland's glorious missionary past. And indeed, in the view of its historian, Edmund Hogan, the establishment of the Maynooth Mission to China did in fact prove to be a watershed in the history of the modern Irish missionary movement, marking it as the moment when the Irish missionary ideal was transformed into action on a large scale.[8]

Following a successful audience in Rome between Pope Benedict XV and Fr Galvin in July 1917, the Vatican eventually approved the allocation to the new society of a mission territory around Hanyang, in Hubei province in central China.

In effect, the Columbans were to have mission responsibility for an area in China about the size of the Irish province of Connaught. Its population of a few million Chinese had only a miniscule Chinese Catholic community. But it was one thing to achieve formal approval, another to give substance to the proposed mission. This process proved as remarkable for the impact it had on Ireland as it had in China. Such was the enthusiasm which was stirred up by the initial half dozen Irish priests of the new society – not only in Ireland but among the Irish diaspora – that their vision was described as 'a new crusade in which Ireland could recapture some of the glories of her missionary past'.[9]

The campaign was extensive and systematic. Fr Blowick, who later became Superior-General of the society, wrote to the Irish bishops seeking their approval for appeals for support to be made at Sunday masses and at diocesan seminaries. Most bishops were very receptive to these requests, facilitating the publicity and fundraising unleashed by Fr Galvin, Fr Blowick, Fr Edward McCarthy and others from late 1916 onwards. According to Fr McCarthy, 'We spend most of our time travelling, by train, sidecar, bicycle … you can guess what it is to go around and interview parish priests, preach three sermons on Sunday, lecture in schools and convents during the week, visit every priest in the diocese as we go along organising lectures etc., [with] not a moment to ourselves.'[10] There was extensive use of the press, which carried promotional features about the new venture. In addition, the society produced a mission magazine, *The Far East*, with early print runs of 10,000 copies. In its first year Fr Blowick reported that on the financial side they had already raised in Ireland a sum of £33,000.[11]

The phenomenal growth of the new society coincided with the nationalist mobilisation in Ireland. Fr Blowick was asked whether he thought the national uprising of Easter 1916 helped the missionary movement. He replied: 'I am strongly of the opinion that the Rising of 1916 helped our work indirectly. I know for a fact that many of the young people of the country had been aroused into a state of heroism and zeal by the Rising of 1916 and by the manner in which the leaders met their death.'[12] This is a plausible view. Fr Edward McCarthy, for example, describing his promotion tour of 1916–17, wrote how 'I was preaching in Carndonagh in the north of Donegal. The parish priest in introducing me said "the next time you will hear of Father McCarthy, he will be martyred in China!" I got £60 there.'[13]

The reality, of course, was that priests in China would be much more likely to die prematurely of ill health than through martyrdom. But it is indicative of how deeply a widespread idealism and its sympathy with martyrdom affected both politically and religiously minded people in Ireland at that time. Nor was this confined to Irish Catholics. The tragic deaths of some of the early Irish Protestant missionaries in China, including the murder of Robert Stewart and his family in 1895 and the drowning of Joseph Collins and his family in 1897, rather than discouraging recruits, in fact inspired more Irish missionaries to seek work in China.

In fact, it has been suggested by the Columban historian Michael O'Neill that the missionary movement provided Irish Catholics an outlet for an idealism untainted by the physical-force Irish nationalism about which the Catholic Church leadership was uncomfortable.[14] But had the Easter Rising never occurred, Hogan insists, the Maynooth Mission would still have succeeded because 'Ireland was already interested in non-Christian missions and capable of profound commitment.'[15]

Abroad, Fr Galvin toured the United States in 1917 and obtained significant support from Irish American bishops. He sought a host diocese for the Columbans in America and in March 1917 secured one at Omaha, Nebraska. He then went downtown, rented a single-room office and put up a sign: 'The Irish Mission to China'.[16] The American base was successful in terms of both fundraising and attracting student priests to the new mission. By 1920 the American edition of the *Far East* magazine had 60,000 subscribers. A Columban centre was also opened in Australia.

In 1918, another pioneer responded to Fr Blowick's call – this time, for women to go to China to work with the priests.

This was Lady Frances Moloney (1873–1959), born in London of Irish background, who, when widowed in 1913, moved from Italy to Ireland and immersed herself in charitable and religious activities. Fr Blowick envisioned a new congregation of nuns whose vow would be the medical care of the sick in China.[17] Lady Moloney and a small band of like-minded women lost no time in enrolling for training in midwifery; she then went in 1920 to London to obtain experience of tropical medicine. Lady Moloney was also generous in financing the costs of the new venture. While their medical training progressed, the arrangements for their religious formation took longer to set up and did not begin until 1922. In the end, Lady Moloney became the co-founder of the Missionary Sisters of Saint Columban.[18] Fr Galvin advised them that the women would need to be both religious and hardy; in his own words: 'women who would be ready at a moment's notice to jump on a horse and ride any distance to a sick call.'[19] By 1926, six Columban Sisters, including Lady Moloney (now Sister Mary Patrick), had arrived in China.

With all this preparatory work, it was not until 1920 that Frs Blowick and Galvin led the first party of Columban missionaries to China and established Ireland's first Catholic Mission territory at Hanyang. **[figure 16]** On 24 October 1920 Fr Galvin recorded: 'Mr Patrick Joseph Wang was baptised by me today – our first baptism in China. Deo Gratias.'[20]

The period of the Columban presence in China coincided with major floods and famine, internal warfare and the Japanese invasion. The Columban priests and sisters made noteworthy contributions to humanitarian aid at these times. Accounts of their work – religious, educational, medical – provided in cooperation with the Chinese, are available elsewhere.[21] Only a brief mention can here be made of the missionary endeavours of other Irish Catholic organisations. One such was the Christian Brothers (who worked alongside the Columbans in Hanyang providing primary schooling) and the Irish Vincentians. Missionary work by the Irish continued until the early 1950s. By that time, due to a radically changed political situation under Communism, all foreign missionaries in China, Protestant and Catholic, were required to leave the country.

In regard to Irish Protestant mission agencies, it is worth noting that in the period before ecumenism and before the Second Vatican Council (1962–65), Protestant and Catholic missionaries were generally wary of each other and had little contact; this was no different for the Irish Catholic and Protestant missionaries in China. This situation is epitomised by the two young idealistic Irish missionaries from west County Cork, one Catholic, Fr Edward Galvin, and one a Methodist, Dr Sally Wolfe,[22] who both worked for decades between the two world wars in the area of Wuhan, apparently oblivious of each other – their particular denominational affiliations and involvements dwarfing their common national geographical origins.

Historically, two Church of Ireland or Anglican mission agencies have also worked in China: the Irish branch of the Church Mission Society, also known as the Hibernian Church Missionary Society (now CMS Ireland), and the Dublin University Far Eastern Mission (DUFEM), founded in Trinity College, Dublin in 1885 as the Dublin University Fukien Mission.[23] The allocation of Fujian Province by CMS to Irish missionaries in 1897 consolidated the identification of the Church of Ireland with work in China.

When the first Anglican missionaries arrived in China in the 1840s they included three graduates of Trinity College Dublin: of these, the most prominent was William Armstrong Russell, the first Irish Anglican bishop in China.[24] A key figure in the formation of an independent Anglican Church in China, the Chung Hua Sheng Kung Hui (CHSKH), Russell was to work with three other Church of Ireland bishops – Herbert James Molony of Zhejiang (Chekiang); John Hind of Fujian (Fukien); and John Curtis of Zhejiang[25] – to move the Church in China from dependence on mission agencies to being truly indigenous and independent.

William Russell (1821–79), originally from Littleton, County Tipperary, left for China in 1847 and worked mainly in Ningbo (Ningpo). When the second Opium War ended in 1859, he was deeply anguished that the humiliating terms of the treaty dictated by Britain had been secured by 'the hand of man, of cruel, covetous, God-less man', and he condemned the events. After the Taiping rebels stormed Ningbo in 1861, Russell, against his better judgement, was recalled to England, where he worked on translating the New Testament and the *Book of Common Prayer* into Chinese. But the call to China came again with proposals for a missionary diocese centred on Ningbo.

Russell's consecration was delayed as the mission agencies argued over diocesan boundaries and the need to free mission work from colonial, trading and political interests in Hong Kong. The new diocese covered all China north of Latitude 28 and included the Anglican missionaries and chaplains working in Shanghai and Beijing. Russell was consecrated the first Bishop of North China in 1872 and set about organising a truly Chinese Church. Missionary work in Beijing was left to the more high church Anglicans from the Society for the Propagation of the Gospel (SPG) and the Episcopal Church of the United States, while Russell focused on a region including Ningbo, Hangzhou and Shanghai, then China's principal port and commercial centre. In 1875, Holy Trinity Church, Shanghai, became the cathedral of his diocese.

Russell wanted a diocese free of the controls of colonial interests in Hong Kong and a Church that did not depend on colonial and imperial expansion for opportunities for growth and evangelism. He wanted the Chinese people to have their own clergy and the Bible and the liturgy in their own language, and these principles would pave the way for an authentically Chinese Church that would be self-propagating, self-supporting and self-governing.

When Russell died in Ningbo in 1879, the Diocese of North China was divided into the Diocese of North China, which was based in Beijing and was transferred to SPG, and the Diocese of Mid-China, based in Shanghai.

Likewise, when Herbert James Molony became Bishop of Mid-China, he too worked to move his diocese from missionary control to being part of a truly Chinese Church. Molony, born in Dublin in 1865, was consecrated bishop in 1908. A year later the names and boundaries of Chinese dioceses were changed and Molony became Bishop of Zhejiang, a diocese that included Hangzhou and Ningbo, as well as the English-speaking congregation of Holy Trinity Cathedral, Shanghai. One of Molony's first moves was to appoint a Chinese priest, Sing Tsae-Seng, as his archdeacon. He began transferring the control of church life in Zhejiang from the missionaries in 1910 when he proposed forming self-supporting Chinese church councils, with diocesan boards taking responsibility for all pastoral work. His proposals were rejected by the mission agencies but were supported by the missionaries in his diocese, who felt the need was for more Chinese catechists and teachers rather than more missionaries.

In 1912, eleven of the twelve Anglican and Episcopalian dioceses in China – the exception was the Diocese of Victoria in Hong Kong – united to form an autonomous Anglican Church, which was named the Chung Hua Sheng Kung Hui (CHSKH, literally the Holy Catholic Church of China): a title that indicated the bishops, clergy and church regarded themselves as closer to Catholic theology, liturgy and practices rather than identifying with Protestants such as Methodists, Presbyterians, Baptists and the China Inland Mission. The name made an important theological point in terms of the Irish ecumenical understanding of the Church as well as within the Chinese context, where Catholics and Protestants had drifted far apart: that being the Anglican's understanding of themselves as a bridge between the two traditions.

In moving the CHSKH towards self-government, independence and indigenisation, Molony played a key role. At its first synod the CHSKH approved its own constitution, strongly influenced by the Church of Ireland. CMS delegates from Europe who visited Zhejiang in 1912–13 were impressed by 'the advanced condition of the organised church life' in Molony's diocese but were unhappy that local committees were organising mission work. However, Molony continued devolving control and transferring property from foreign missions to the local church. A conference in Hangzhou in 1917 accepted his request for a Chinese assistant bishop, and accordingly Archdeacon Sing Tsae-Seng was consecrated in 1918.

In 1921, the CHSKH sought recognition as a self-governing Church within the Anglican Communion. However, Molony's desire to transfer his diocese from the control of foreign-born missionaries to local church leaders was opposed by many missionaries, who said he had 'killed evangelism' or that he was power-seeking and authoritarian. However by the time Molony retired in 1928, he had transferred most CMS property, including churches, schools and hospitals, to the diocese.

In much the same way, the Belfast-born Bishop of Fujian, John Hind (1879–1958), saw the need for the Church in China to become authentically Chinese. In fact, his vision and his theology of mission and of the Church prefigured many of the theological foundations for the Church in China today. As a student at Trinity College, Dublin, Hind was already active in DUFEM. When he was ordained in Hong Kong in 1903, he was given oversight of Funing district and its parishes. He travelled throughout Funing on foot or in the *TCD*, a small boat presented to the mission by Trinity College, Dublin. But, following the death of his wife and their first child, Hind returned to Belfast with their surviving baby son. Then, against all expectations, he returned to China in 1911, just as Sun Yat-sen's revolution was bringing down the old imperial order. Back in Fuzhou, he became headmaster of the CMS Middle School in Fuzhou and worked at Trinity College Fuzhou, founded in 1907 by missionaries from Trinity College, Dublin.

In 1918, Hind was appointed Bishop of Fujian (Fuzhou), which was formed as a new, separate diocese out of the Diocese of Hong Kong in 1906. As bishop, he lived in Nantai Island, to the south of Fuzhou, the location of many foreign consulates, schools and churches. His diocese was slightly larger than Ireland: with 38,500 square miles and (out of a population of over 4 million) about 18,000 Christians and 280 Anglican congregations. He spoke of his 'deep concern to see the Church become more truly Chinese in character and to see the administration become Church-centric rather than mission-centric'.[26] In fact, a mass movement to Christianity spread so rapidly among the fishing community and boat people of the Funing Coast that, when he came to confirm the baptised, they and their friends were so numerous the service was held in the open air.

At his first diocesan synod in 1919, Hind ended the custom of keeping minutes in English and insisted that all speeches be in Chinese. Convinced that the mission to China must become the Church in China, he reversed the accepted seniority of the missionaries, who were now to become assistants to Chinese incumbents or clergy. The missionaries no longer chaired church councils, and decisions about where they worked were transferred to the diocesan synod. With this agenda in mind, Hind played a crucial ecumenical role at the National Christian Conference in Shanghai in 1922, which led to the formation of the National Christian Council of China, the predecessor of today's China Christian Council. He recognised how Chinese Christians resented 'the control of Christian activities by missions and missionaries' and hoped that 'gradually and one by one, the present institutions are replaced by institutions which bear a fully indigenous character'.[27] Hind's agenda began to be realised when, in 1927, Archdeacon Ding Ingong was consecrated in Shanghai Cathedral as Hind's assistant – the first Chinese assistant bishop in the diocese. When Hind left for England (to undergo a major operation as well as to attend the 1930 Lambeth Conference), Bishop Ding was in charge of the diocese for two years. Hind later said this prolonged absence 'helped ... to forward the purpose which was one of the chief aims of my episcopate – namely, the development of a truly indigenous Church'.[28]

In the 1930s, Fuzhou was bombed by the Japanese; schools, hospitals and roads were destroyed, and famine was widespread. Hind realised the time had come to hand over to a Chinese successor, and he and Ding retired in 1940. Hind retained an active interest in the Church in China, publishing his *Fukien Memories* in Belfast in 1951.[29] He died in Belfast in 1958.

John Curtis (1880–1962), the last Irish Anglican bishop to work in China, had a similar vision of a Church that was truly independent and truly Chinese, prefiguring much of contemporary

Chinese theology. Curtis, who was born in Dublin, was once an Irish soccer international. He first worked in China in Fujian (1906–28), and after Molony retired as Bishop of Zhejiang, Curtis was consecrated as his successor in 1929. The diocese covered 36,680 square miles and by 1950 had a population of 23 million, of whom 11,574 were Anglicans. The diocese also included 3,000 Anglicans in the so-called English congregations in Shanghai, along with Holy Trinity Cathedral, Shanghai. As bishop, Curtis lived in Hangzhou; from there he worked to integrate mission work into the life of his diocese, incorporating the Chinese CMS into the diocesan board of missions in 1930. Despite civil war and famine, Curtis remained in his diocese. 'In his long journeys about his diocese, mainly on foot, he was a hard man to follow,' the Dean of Shanghai recalled later. 'In a New Year's sermon in the cathedral, with an unconscious Irishness, he urged us to "advance in all directions".'[30]

Japanese invaders stormed Hangzhou on Christmas Day 1937. As living conditions in the city deteriorated, Curtis constantly visited the hospitals, medical camps and refugees, his coat pockets bulging with bottles of milk for the children. During those 'milk rounds', he helped large numbers of frightened women and children to safety in the refugee camps. As Curtis repeatedly toured the diocese, the Church continued to grow. By 1940, the number of baptised Anglicans in the diocese was 12,000 – more than double those in 1920. When Curtis was finally detained in Shanghai in 1942 and then in Hong Kong, the Japanese threatened to shoot him if he persisted in criticising their treatment of prisoners; nevertheless he continued to work to maintain the morale of his fellow inmates.

After World War II, Curtis fretted: 'We are further away from self-help now than when I came here [Hangzhou] 17 years ago.' But at the end of his career he had a larger vision, saying, 'We are passing from mission relationships to Church relationships.' Eventually, he left China in 1950 at the age of 70. A CMS missionary recalled that, as a bishop, Curtis displayed 'distinctively Irish gifts' that were valued in non-Anglican ecumenical circles which had little use for bishops.[31]

China *and the* Irish

The experience of the disestablishment in Ireland of the Church of Ireland in 1870 may have been instrumental for Irish Anglicans in China in encouraging them to support an independent, self-governing Chinese Church that would control the work of missionaries and mission agencies. The three self-principles of a church that is self-supporting, self-governing and self-propagating, first framed by missionaries such as Henry Venn and Roland Allen, as applied by Russell, Hind, Molony and Curtis, now underpin the ecclesiology of the Three-Self Patriotic Movement, which emerged in the 1950s, and that of the China Christian Council, formed in 1980.[32]

Among the other Irish Protestant denominations, Presbyterian missionaries in China included: the Revd William Proctor, later Minister of the Scots' Church, Dublin; the Revd Robert Knox Lyle, a former Irish rugby international, who returned to become the Presbyterian minister in Enniscorthy, Wexford, and Greystones; and the Revd Thomas Blakeley, who left China at the same time as John Curtis and became minister of Trinity Presbyterian Church, Cork.[33] Dr Jack Weir, born in China in 1909 of missionary parents, worked as a missionary in China and later became the Moderator and General Secretary of the Presbyterian Church in Ireland. In particular, Irish Methodist missionaries in China were noted for their commitment to medical work. The Revd Dr Robert Booth from Cork worked in Hankou (Wuhan) from 1898–1912 and helped establish the Red Cross in China. He was followed to China by Dr Richard Hadden and Dr George Hadden from Wexford and George Hadden's wife, Dr Helen Hadden. John and Deirdre Fee were arrested by the Japanese in 1941, but their Irish citizenship saved them from being treated as prisoners of war.[34] Revd Desmond Gilliland with his wife Kit Cundall continued the Irish Methodist missionary presence between 1946 and 1950.

In the early decades of Communist Party rule religious practice was greatly restricted. All foreign missionaries in China, Protestant and Catholic, were required to leave the country. But since the death of Mao in 1976, much (but not full) religious freedom has been restored, with many former churches reopening.[35] Curtis's Hangzhou has again a lively church life, its Chong-yi Church being the largest in China. Holy Trinity Cathedral, the former Anglican cathedral in Shanghai used by the Irish bishops, has been handed back to the Church. Some Columban Fathers and Sisters and other individual Irish Christians have been able to return to China, this time as English-language teachers.

As is clear from this short history, the Irish Christian missionary involvement with China was diverse in terms of denominational composition and contributions. However, despite sectarian devisions, it made a significant impact on both China and on Ireland. On the Catholic side, there was the remarkable sudden impact in Ireland itself and on the Irish diaspora through the mobilisation of interest in the Church in China and the development of a major new indigenous Irish Catholic foreign mission to the Far East. On the Irish Anglican side, there has been a singular contribution to the development in China of a truly indigenous and independent Christian Church.

Finally, having pursued separate missionary activity in China during the twentieth century, the Irish missionary organisations in China, notably DUFEM and the Columbans, are now entering a new era as they respond, in their own communities, to some thousands of mainland Chinese students and workers who, in the opening years of the twenty-first century, have now come to live in Ireland.[36]

.8.

Musical
Meetings,
East and West:

The Chieftains in China

✫

Hwee-San Tan

In 1983 an Irish traditional music group, The Chieftains, played
in China. They were among the first from the West to perform
there following the close of the Cultural Revolution period.
Playing in Beijing and other cities, they not only toured on their
own, but also performed with Chinese folk musicians. So successful was this informal collaboration that Paddy Maloney, leader
of the Chieftains, stated that he believed, at some point in time,
'what has become identifiable as Chinese traditional music
crossed with the early foundation of Irish music, as one moved
east, the other moved west'.[1] Maloney's observation is far more
astute than he perhaps realises, for there are many uncanny
similarities between the traditional musical practices of both

countries. As if to prove this hypothesis, since their visit to China, The Chieftains have often played well-loved Chinese folk tunes such as 'Full of Joy' (*Xi Yangyang*) in their live performances in Ireland and elsewhere, using an array of both Chinese and Irish traditional instruments in their rendition.

Yet the musics of these two cultures are rarely thought of as having much in common; indeed, they are assumed to be highly culturally specific. So how is it that the Irish musicians could play Chinese music without great difficulty? What traits do these two musics share that allow such collaboration between their musicians? And how different or similar in practice and performance are these music systems?

In part, the answer lies in the Westernisation and modernisation of Chinese music. But to explore how this happened, we must first ask: what is Chinese music? And how has it been traditionally practised?

China is a country with a long, ancient civilisation. Archaeological excavations of tombs from more than two millennia ago have unearthed musical instruments such as zithers and mouth organs whose descendants are still played today. However, Chinese music has not been frozen in time but has constantly evolved. Over many centuries, that major route between East and West, the Silk Road, enriched the culture and specifically the music of China. Folk instruments of today which are considered traditionally Chinese, including the four-string lute, hammered dulcimer, reed-pipes, shawms and bronze percussion instruments, came over the Silk Road from the Middle East via Central Asia. These instruments have been assimilated and gradually sinicised to become an intrinsic part of Chinese music. And, in this globalised age, the contact with the Western world continues to breathe life into Chinese music, as epitomised by The Chieftains' interaction with Chinese folk musicians.

So what, then, is 'Chinese music'? 'Chinese music' is really a misnomer as that term implies a single entity. In fact, the multiethnic composition of China yields many different types of music and musical traditions. Music of the Han Chinese alone comprises many different genres and styles suitable to different needs and contexts. This essay will deal only with the music of the Han Chinese and specifically their instrumental music.[2]

To many people in the West, the stereotypical notion of the Chinese musical scale is that it is pentatonic, or to put it in layman's words, the scale sounds like the five black keys on the piano. In solfege, the five tones are *sol, la, do, re, mi.* Pentatonicism is also regarded as a common trait in music of the Far East (China, Japan and Korea) and Southeast Asia (Java, Bali, Thailand and so on) and as being less common in Europe. But pentatonicism is, in fact, not unknown in Irish music. Through deciphering the older method of tuning the Irish harp, Irish music scholars have actually found that early Irish music also favoured the pentatonic scale.[3]

Similarly, just like the Chinese, Irish harp music might add a sixth or seventh tone to the scale. Thus, it is not unusual to hear the *re* and *fa*, the second and seventh degrees of the scale; but, at the same time, these are often subsidiary to the other five tones. In Chinese music, these two degrees may function as passing or neighbouring tones in a melody. In the Chinese case, however, the second and seventh degrees also have a more important function of indicating a particular mode or facilitating the change of modes, or heightening the tension between different modes. It was noted that early Irish melodies preferred a lowered or flattened seventh note when used.[4] In most Chinese genres, the fourth degree is often slightly higher and the seventh lower than in the Western diatonic scale. This is where specific cultural and aesthetic choices come into play.

China's seven-string *qin* zither is one of the oldest indigenous Chinese instruments still played today. An elongated wooden box with seven strings stretched lengthwise across the main body, it is a fretless instrument. The player plucks the strings with the right-hand fingers near the right end of the surface, while the left-hand fingers move or slide along the entire board to make stopped notes. The form of the instrument as we know it today dates back to the late third century AD. Rich lore and cosmological significance surrounding the instrument and its association with the lofty and reclusive Confucian literati elevated its position to a

high spiritual and intellectual level. It has its own unique nota-
tional system, the oldest surviving notations dating from around
the fifteenth century. The music of the *qin* is predominantly pentatonic, the five tones being recognised in classical music treatises
as the 'orthodox sounds' (*zhengsheng*). The strings are tuned to
several different pentatonic modes depending on the piece. As
with many other Chinese instruments before the influences of
Westernisation, the tuning of the *qin* is unlike Western equal temperament. (I will return to this below when discussing van Aalst's
writings.) Equally, Annie W. Patterson wrote that in ancient Irish
music 'just intonation has no existence upon our keyboard instruments, and that a tempered, and, shall we confess it, *artificial* scale
system has taken the place of nature's gamut'.[5]

While the music of the *qin* is predominantly pentatonic, many
genres of Chinese instrumental music frequently use the hepta-
tonic seven-tone scale – for example, the *pipa* four-string lute. Its
ancestor was brought from Persia via the Silk Route during the
fifth century. It has since adapted and evolved, becoming an
intrinsically Chinese instrument. Frequently, the fourth and
seventh tones provide tonal colouring and modal variation.

Thus, I hope to have dispelled the myth that Chinese music
has only five tones: seven tones are just as commonly used.
Some genres of Irish music also once favoured pentatonicism,
as mentioned earlier, but seven-note pieces predominate today.
Preferences for musical temperament other than the Western
equal-tempered one also at one time existed in both cultures.
At a superficial level, these elements could be seen as similarities. However, at a deeper level, each culture has different
conceptions and preferences for the way they construct their
melodic modes.

Yet, if deeper structural differences exist between the two
musics, what else is there that facilitates the meeting of the two
cultures musically? This brings me to the next topic: performance practice and transmission.

Traditionally, the repertoires of most Chinese folk music are
built upon a system known as *qupai* which are 'labelled' melodies
with names or titles, comprising, in their most basic form, short

tunes of fixed beat-count, the lengths of which may vary between 24 and 68 beats for the most common tunes. These became the basis for generating the musical repertoires of most Chinese musical genres.

Most 'labelled melodies' took their name from an associated original song text. A melody with a title has a known melodic outline (often referred to as the skeletal melody). When played in this most basic form, it is usually in a fast tempo. However, the 'labelled melody' is often expanded through different types of variation techniques. Melodic decoration or ornamentation is one way of dressing up the nuclear or skeletal melodies. One common technique of variation in Chinese music is the slowing down of the tempo, thus expanding the beats and allowing dense ornamentation to fill the space between the original melody notes. Rhythmic subdivisions are also interpolated.

When expanded temporally, a piece of 'labelled melody' can be so densely decorated that its original version is often quite obscure to an 'untuned' ear. In this way, one could say that a new piece is created. Indeed, this is one of the methods of composition in traditional Chinese folk music. The repertory has grown from use of old tunes as structural models and the application of variation techniques in the creation of new pieces. At other times, the 'labelled melody' may be retained in suite-like pieces, usually emerging toward the end of the piece as it moves from the slow, expanded and heavily ornamented version to a less ornamented medium-tempo variation and finally to the fast, unornamented skeletal tune. Different 'labelled melodies' can also be put together in instrumental suites. Thus it can be said that *qupai* are the basic building block of music all over China. Nonetheless, the resulting music is not homogenous: regional variations and sub-cultural musical idioms ensure that the musical legacy is one of rich diversity.

In the late-nineteenth century, van Aalst, author of the book entitled *Chinese Music*, written by order of Inspector General Robert Hart, observed the following about Chinese ensemble playing:

> The orchestra ordinarily consists of two balloon-shaped guitars (played by girls who sing at the same time), one

three-stringed guitar, one or two violins, one small drum
to beat time, one flute, and one *yang-qin* [a hammered
dulcimer]. All these instruments play, or at least try to play,
in unison; still it seems to a foreigner not acquainted with
their music that each performer has a part of his own, and
that each aims to distinguish himself above his colleagues
by making as much noise as he can. The impression
produced on foreign ears is anything but favourable. Still,
if patient attention is paid, it is soon discovered that the
performers play in time and well together.[6]

Van Aalst is indeed right about each performer having a part
of their own. An aesthetic sensibility of Chinese ensemble music
is individual variation during performance. A technical term for
this type of performance practice is *heterophony*: the simultaneous
variation of the same melody by each of the different instruments,
giving the impression of a sort of loose unison.

This type of micro-level variation-making is common
throughout Chinese music, and indeed ethnomusicologists have
found this to be common practice in many of the world's traditions, Irish music included. Ornamentation, variation in melodic
and rhythmic patterns, articulation and phrasing are very much a
part of the performance practice of traditional Irish music. Similar
to the Chinese, Irish musicians also develop melodic and
rhythmic variations based on the framework of a tune.[7]

In the instrumental Silk and Bamboo (*sizhu*) ensemble
tradition of the Shanghai region, amateur music clubs flourish in
public tea houses. This type of ensemble draws its name from its
instruments, which are made of bamboo or have strings traditionally made from silk; they include the three- and four-string
lutes, transverse and vertical bamboo flutes, mouth organ, two-
string fiddle and wooden clappers and drum. Members generally
meet weekly to perform. One could certainly draw a parallel with
sessions in Irish pubs. Just as in pub sessions, Silk and Bamboo
musicians perform from memory, each player embellishing and
interpreting the same melodic framework according to idiomatic
practices of each instrument. The aesthetic aim is therefore to

'include the making of spontaneous musical choices at a relatively "micro level"'.[8]

I believe that The Chieftains could play at ease with folk
musicians in China and vice versa precisely because of their
familiarity with this kind of performance practice. A YouTube
recording[9] featuring The Chieftains playing the Chinese tune
'Full of Joy' in a concert in Belfast in 1991 demonstrates the
ease with which they grasp the ethos of Chinese musical performance practice, mixing Irish musical instruments with
Chinese percussion and a *yangqin* hammered dulcimer, embellishing the tune with their own musical idiom and yet
successfully sounding authentically Chinese. This is partial
evidence of the similarity of certain characteristics of the two
musics that allows for collaboration between musicians of the
two cultures.

This form of performance practice is built really on the basis
of oral transmission. Traditionally, in both China and Ireland,
music and musical practices are transmitted orally, often within
the family and from generation to generation. Due to modernisation, colonisation and Westernisation, music and its practice in
both of these countries have not escaped the myriad forces of
change. Certainly, China's contact with the West has resulted in
some changes in its musical system, and indeed these have
brought its music closer to that of the West.

China's contact with Ireland began with Irishmen who served
in the British imperial service. One of the most important was Sir
Robert Hart: Chief Inspector-General of Chinese Customs and
a key figure in the introduction of both Western music to China
and of Chinese music to the West.

As is related in essay three in this series, Robert Hart was
appointed to the British Foreign Office for Consular Service in
China in 1854, entering the newly established Chinese Imperial
Maritime Customs. In 1863, he was appointed Inspector-General.
From then on, Hart devoted all his life to the service, returning
to Ireland only in 1908 at age of 73.

Although Hart did not have formal lessons with a teacher, he
learnt the violin and cello and played them well. He loved

music, and his correspondence with James Duncan Campbell, his agent in London, was dotted with requests to find specific musical scores, violin strings, instruments and other musical items. After his wife left China in 1881 with their children to live in London, Hart devoted much of his spare time to music, seeking out subordinates who had musical skills. In a letter to Campbell in 1885, he wrote: 'My surroundings now are very musical: Scherzer and Liot: piano; Lyall: violin; van Aalst: piano, flute, Hautboy; self: violin and cello; and we have every Saturday a musical dinner party.'[10] Apart from music-making, Hart was also a keen composer: he wrote ten songs and ten pieces for the violin, and even thought of publishing them, urging Campbell to find an able composer to provide piano accompaniment to his pieces.[11]

One of Hart's most significant contributions to the Westernisation of music in China was to set up the first-ever Western brass band in China. The idea of starting a brass band came to Hart in April 1890. Using his own money to buy instruments and musical scores from England, Hart also wrote to ask Campbell to keep an eye open for a '*good* Brass-instrument man, who would make a good Postal-clerk and good Bandmaster'.[12] Soon after, the Commissioner of Customs in Tianjin (Tientsin) wrote to Hart to say that one of his postmasters, a Portuguese by the name of E.E. Encarnaçao, was a fine bandmaster. Encarnaçao was duly appointed the leader of the band and helped to recruit at least a dozen young Chinese in Beijing into the band. Among the recruits were the following:

> a promising barber, lured, perhaps by the playing of his friend's flute, abandoned his trade and set to work on the cello; or a shoemaker, forsaking his last, devoted himself to the cornet. The neighbouring tailor laid aside his needle; the carter left his cart, bewitched away from everyday things by the music.[13]

Under the leadership of Encarnaçao, the young recruits learnt very quickly, and within a year several of them were ready to teach others. **[figure 17]** The number of bands expanded rapidly in Beijing, Tianjin, Shanghai and other cities. By the 1930s, brass bands began to appear in Chinese films and also in funerals.[14] Hart's band in Beijing reached such a standard that his musicians were playing open-air concerts in the Inspectorate garden once a week, drawing local Beijing residents as well as foreigners. The band certainly became a constant backdrop for the numerous garden parties Hart threw. Even the Empress Dowager specially commanded their performance at the Summer Palace in 1903. Hart told Campbell: 'the "boys" are in great glee over the prospects of visiting the Summer Palace and playing for emperor and court, Encarnaçao goes with them: I hope he will get a [order of] "double dragon" out of it.'[15] His band of Chinese musicians playing Western music certainly became one of the major curiosities of Beijing; another being Inspector-General Hart himself.

Apart from nurturing Western brass bands, in 1890 Hart also went about setting up 'by my own teaching and for my own amusement – a *stringed quartette*'.[16] He was going to pick out five or six of the brightest of his fifteen brass-band musicians to learn the cello, violin and viola. From the numerous concert programmes in the Hart Archive, we can see that his string band was a huge success and was often put to good use, providing music for the numerous balls and dances hosted by Hart, and even for the conferring ceremonies at Peking University where Hart was a member of the Board of Managers. **[figure 18]**

Hart was equally curious about and supportive of *Chinese* music studies. Among one of the earliest Western writings on Chinese music well known to Chinese music researchers is the book by the Belgian J. A. van Aalst (mentioned above as one of Hart's musicians). Van Aalst was one of the many foreigners working for the Chinese Imperial Maritime Customs and part of Hart's Saturday musical party. Indeed, his book on Chinese music, published in 1884 by the Statistical Department of the Inspectorate General, was 'by order of the Inspector General of Customs'. The book was probably published to coincide with the Health Exhibition in London in the same year, to which van Aalst was sent by Hart to deliver a lecture on Chinese music. In his instructions to Campbell about the set-up for the Health Exhibition, Hart wrote:

> We shall also probably send you a good essay or lecture on Chinese education (which Hippisley will provide) and another on Chinese music by van Aalst. You will have to read the former, and possibly van Aalst may go as one of the secretaries and read the latter – more especially if I can induce a Chinese string band (to make music in the restaurant and torture the London ear with the delights of Chinese daily life).[17]

For the event, Hart succeeded in sending six Chinese opera performers who could 'act, sing and play musical instruments', in what was probably the first Chinese musical exchange with Britain.[18] Robert Campbell wrote in a memoir of his father, James Duncan Campbell:

> When it first arrived this band could only play Chinese music, which, though regarded by some experts [probably referring to van Aalst] as akin to the music of ancient Greece, grated strangely on English ears. But under the guidance of Dr Wilde, Gresham Professor of Music and head of the London Academy of Music, the band speedily mastered most of the popular English airs and, of course, the various national anthems, and its daily performances in a Chinese pavilion built over an artificial lake were warmly cheered by admiring audiences.[19]

Thus Hart, an Irishman who lived more than half his life in China, played a key role in the introduction of Chinese music to the West and also Western music and musical instruments to the Chinese.

Prior to this, however, the Jesuits had been the main intermediaries between China and the West. In the late-seventeenth century, Jesuit missionaries (who had begun their work in China almost a century earlier) presented the Qing emperor Kangxi with a spinet. Delighted by the gift, the emperor ordered four of his musical eunuchs to learn the instrument. A junior priest named Pantoja was put in charge and travelled daily to the palace to teach the eunuchs. The Jesuits even composed 'Eight Short Songs in Chinese', based on texts with moral and religious themes, but this music did not survive. In the 1690s Kangxi wrote: '[The Jesuit] Pereira taught me to play the tune "*p'u yen-chou*" on the harpsichord and the structure of the eight-note scale. Pedrini taught my sons musical theory, and Gheradini painted portraits at the court.'[20] The tune referred to by Kangxi is a well-known *qin* piece 'The Incantation of Pu'an' (*Pu'an zhou*). This attests to the fact that not only were the Jesuits imparting knowledge of Western music to the emperor and his sons, but they also learnt and knew Chinese music well. Other Jesuit priests who contributed to the exchange of musical knowledge included Amiot,[21] Laborde and du Halde.[22] Through them, Chinese music and transcriptions of melodies were imparted to the West, contributing to the musical Orientalism and exoticism in Western music in the nineteenth century and after. Puccini, Weber, Hindemith and others adapted Chinese tunes in their compositions. Puccini's *Turandot* is one of the best-known examples, using the Chinese folk song 'Jasmine Flower' (*Molihua*) as a theme throughout the opera.

Although the Jesuits contributed greatly to the exchange of Chinese and Western music, it was not until the twentieth century that Republican China was ready to respond to the stimulus of Westernisation and modernisation. So one might say that Hart's musical activities helped pave the way for the Westernisation of Chinese music. The May Fourth Movement in 1919, paradoxically anti-imperialist, nurtured the new culture movement and gave birth to Chinese Nationalism. Traditional culture and music were seen as a stumbling block to China's modern progress and were therefore, in the eyes of the Chinese themselves, in need of improvement. The first National College of Music (now the Shanghai Conservatory of Music), modelled after the Leipzig Conservatory of Music, was established by the Chinese composer Cai Yuanpei in Shanghai in 1927. Western and

Western-style music was now also taught in schools. This period saw the 'adaptation and improvement' (translating the Chinese word *gailiang*) of musical instruments. The Chinese genuinely felt that by improving the instruments they were also improving and thus modernising Chinese music. This led to extensive standardisation of instruments, often in a direction bringing them closer to Western aesthetic values.

Furthermore, with the return to China of composers and musicians trained in Europe (as well as in European-influenced Japan) in the early 1920s and 1930s, the adoption of Western intonation, harmony, tone colour and use of notation in performance began to infiltrate the Chinese musical system. This further led to the birth of the large modern Chinese orchestra, modelled on the Western symphony orchestra. Traditionally, Chinese ensembles were often small to medium in size, and low-pitched instruments were uncommon. With Western influence, newly adapted instruments imitating the cello and double-bass began to appear. In some instances, Western low-pitched wind or string instruments were directly adopted into Chinese ensembles to provide sonority. In standardising their musical instruments for the modern Chinese orchestra, the Chinese also adopted the Western equal-tempered scale. Van Aalst, upon studying the Chinese method of the division of the scale, summed it up thus:

> By the above table [where he demonstrates the difference between the Chinese 12 semitones and the Western equal-tempered 12 tones] it is seen that while the base and the fifth perfectly agree, all the other notes of the Chinese scale are too sharp, and consequently could not possibly be rendered on our Western tempered instruments. Besides, the octave is so high as to be very unpleasing to our Western ears. This is the principal reason why Chinese music does not leave a better impression on the minds of foreigners.[23]

This was confirmed also by Robert Campbell who earlier had commented that Chinese music 'grated strangely on English ears'.[24] The tuning system was indeed a concern for Chinese musicologists in the modern period. One scholar wrote in the 1950s:

> Using the Chinese temperament can better express national characteristics. But from the viewpoint of progress, the traditional temperament does not suit modern national ideas. Modern compositions require complex changes in tonality. Traditional temperament cannot solve this problem. The twelve-step equal temperament possesses other good qualities also. So, the adoption of the twelve-tone equal temperament is the necessary road we must now take.[25]

In sum, we can see that the Chinese musical system from the latter half of the twentieth century underwent extensive change to become more aligned with Western music. In my opinion, this is also one of the reasons why Irish musicians such as The Chieftains could play with Chinese folk musicians without many problems. If The Chieftains had been in China during Hart and van Aalst's time, they would have encountered greater difficulty in achieving musical harmony. That The Chieftains' success at improvising *à la chinoise* is not merely a result of their musical talent but truly reflects some commonalities between the music systems is supported by Martin Stokes's description of a jam session between skilled Irish and Turkish musicians – which was unsuccessful because, he proposes, the music systems were too different.[26]

Thus we may conclude that there are more commonalities between Irish and Chinese music than one might at first think. Visitors to China today will find pop songs not unlike those in the West everywhere: on the street, in shopping malls, on television and radio. We may think that this is the result of today's globalisation and the influence of the West; but in fact, China's contact with Western music goes back to as early as the seventeenth century, and by the mid-twentieth century, China was adopting many of the most basic features of Western music. Ireland, though a small country, has done its fair share of exerting this Western influence on China through exceptional figures such as Robert Hart and numerous unnamed missionaries. Today this musical exchange flows on as musical groups from the two countries continue to interact. In October 2007, when the first international Chinese music conference to be held in Ireland took place in University College Dublin,[27] informal musical interactions occurred between Chinese scholars/musicians and local Irish musicians. Doubtless this will not be the last of the musical interactions between Ireland and China, and with the increasing presence of Chinese immigrants in Ireland, one certainly hopes that such musical meetings will continue to blossom.

.9.

*Piercing
the
Chinese Veil*

✮

RICHARD BARRETT
CEO, Treasury Holdings

This talk is entitled 'Piercing the Chinese Veil' because China, to a Western mind, evokes images of different cultures, languages, food, habits and therefore a sense of impenetrability. The peoples of the East, to us, are somewhat inscrutable. That derives in part from their vision of themselves as being different from our vision of them. In Mandarin, the name for China is *Zhong Guo*, the English translation of which is 'Middle Kingdom' and the English meaning of which is 'Kingdom in the Centre of the Earth'. Chinese maps show China at the earth's centre – in complete contrast to the maps we are acquainted with in Europe or the USA (which show us in the centre). The pictorial image is indicative of attitude. But, then again, that attitude of the world as revolving around you (rather than you being part of a revolving world) is not proprietary to China – it is absolutely endemic in the United States, United Kingdom and France and everywhere else in the world.

Penetrating a society such as China that perceives itself thus, with its myriad differences of foods, tongues, cultures and traditions, is a matter on which, to attain success, specific and targeted business psychologies must be brought to bear. For, in China, the Western sequence of mapping out

- first, a target;
- second, a route to get there together with strategies of game play and incremental price bidding;
- then a starting point
- and, finally, working backwards from the goal to be achieved

is not a process likely to bring success in China, where results are the culmination of a different process: that of relationship-forming. The formula in China is then much simpler in the broader perspective of

- first, setting a target
- for which the starting point is that of relationship-forming.

Nothing in China can be done except through relationships; forget the Western notion of chequebook diplomacy or acquisition. And, however complex this form of doing business may seem, the methodology of the relationship formation is even more complex.

We have read, earlier in this series of essays, of the mission of the Irishman Lord Macartney to China in 1793 to attempt to export British goods. This expedition was foiled by the failure of the two countries to find a common ground upon which to set aside national self-interests (then manifesting themselves in robust protectionism, which in an Irish context led to the Act of Union). The Chinese have a saying (most often invoked to describe the failure of Sino-Foreign joint ventures): 'Same bed; different dreams'. If the parties seeking to establish commercial relationships do not clearly agree on their relationship goals and each tries to ensure he achieves only his own objectives from those goals, then, in China, you will go the way of Lord Macartney – back to where you came from: with your tail between your legs and at the loss of much time and expenditure of money.

But perhaps one should first ask: what lessons does this ancient society have for us in the evolution of better business practice?

The first point to note is that the notion of the current resurgence of China as being a recent economic event is grossly mistaken. China is only en route to once again taking its premier seat in the first row of nations. In 1300, India and China had 50 per cent of the world's trade. China then dwarfed Europe. Iron manufacture then was 125,000 tonnes per annum, a level not reached in Europe until four centuries later. The vast land area of China was connected by an intricate canal-based transportation structure; trade was conducted on a highly developed paper-money and credit-facility system. China, then, is not just on the way up; she's on the way back.

What are the forces that cause this extraordinary return to the economic spotlight? What makes China an attractive place to do business in? It might be interesting to reflect on these factors to frame the context of how you do business there.

China is an extraordinarily attractive place in which to invest. It is currently dominating world trade. It has a huge Current Account surplus; the world's largest (by far) foreign exchange reserves. It makes commodity prices at the margin – fully 50 per cent of the marginal growth in demand for oil is China-based: for which read, China sets the oil price. As China does the prices of copper, steel, iron ore, tin, lead, zinc, aluminium and a host of other commodities, all fuelling the voracious appetite of China's economic engine, the world's largest trader producing goods at the lowest possible prices.

And so it comes to pass that China is Mr Lowest Cost Producer through a combination of huge economies of scale, the cluster effect of similar industries, an abundant supply of cheap labour and the most modern efficient plants, created by an avalanche of capital, both foreign and Chinese. The falling cost of production of goods, intensified by a transfer of global production to China, causes a fall in the price of consumer goods in the West. The consequent liquidity generated from these vast sales receipts allows China to reciprocate by investing trade surpluses in US Treasury bills and so happily produce the dual benefits of cheaper goods and cheaper credit, which in turn fuels demand for more goods in foreign countries, thus making China even more dominant. A virtuous economic circle, not currently vicious.

Thus in terms of China, you're talking about the world's third largest economy (second, if judged by purchasing power parity), its fastest growing economy for the last 30 years, the largest FDI recipient, the largest exporter, the fourth largest stockmarket, the third largest market for luxury goods (destined to be the largest) and the largest population for any country in the world.

What makes China even more attractive to invest in is the unique policy stability that comes from their particular political system. Western democracies are overprone to policy U-turns for electoral advantage. In the West, as an election approaches, you get either policy *rigor mortis* or policy diarrhoea either side of an election, followed by God knows what policy reversal by the inexperienced incomers if there is a change of the political guard.

Not so in China, where only consummately skilled persons in government reach the top and they can't reach the top without lifelong training. This allows the Long View to be taken by Long Viewers, a benefit best exhibited by the quite extraordinary scale of advance infrastructure provision by the Chinese government. Whether it's Maglev or bullet trains, the thousands of kilometres of highways, the enormous provision of metro systems at colossal cost, the creation and expansion of so many airports – this government saw the future and constructed the physical infra-structure to support it (a factor that both attracts investment and wins it competitively). China wins hands down over India because of that – India's infrastructure and squabbling politicians (unsure of how long they'll be there) could never match these Chinese advantages. In October of 2007 the composition of this was uniquely suited to large-scale long-term capital expenditures with very long payback periods: the core leadership then composed of eight engineers and a geologist; now seven engineers, one geologist and an economist. With no distracting electoral events, capital could be deployed where it would not have been in less long-sighted jurisdictions (as, for instance, in countries with five-year electoral cycles, where capital investment decisions are made by reference to their capacity to produce a return in the life of the deciding government).

And China is clearly the beneficiary of the stupendous scale of such far-sighted decisions. Watch for the future when corporations will place plants in China because of the existence of such infrastructure rather than in allegedly advanced rival nations such as the US or the UK. Democratic values are to be cherished, but, sometimes, democracies and the way their political systems operate in practice makes democracies themselves (as opposed to the democratic values they represent) less than commercially efficient. The best anecdote on the Long View that I know is the question asked of Zhou Enlai, Chinese Premier from 1949 to the early 70s. When asked what he thought of Napoleon's march on Moscow in 1812 and the lessons to be learned from that debacle, he replied that it was 'Too early yet to be able to understand its full significance.'

And now this country is willing to accept your money and happy that you benefit from your investment. Ever since Deng Xiaoping's critical tour of South China in 1992, when he rescued the Chinese people from economic oblivion, his mantra of 'To be rich is glorious' (mirrored in the Chinese New Year greeting *Gongxi facai*: 'Congratulations on getting rich') has been adopted with gusto by the Chinese people, who have, in the process, invented a peculiarly Communist form of quasi-capitalism that, in some respects, works better than its Western counterpart.

So this very attractive prize of getting a piece of Chinese action beckons, as it now does to the whole world. How do you get it?

RICHARD BARRETT

At the start of this essay, I referred to the formation of relationships and the understanding of what the other party's objectives are from that relationship as key parameters to success in a culture as different from ours as can be imagined. This difference in culture is profound and failure awaits those who think that business in China is, or can be conducted, as it is in the West.

The basis for the cultural differences are, not surprisingly, reflections of fundamental values within a larger Chinese society. Though mostly religionless for many years, China had for more than two millennia adopted the moral code of Confucian behaviour, a philosophy that is based upon mutual reciprocal good.

This has also influenced modes of thought. Chinese tend to focus on context and relationships; Westerners on individual details and abstract categories. Chinese and European children shown pictures of a hen, a cow and grass when asked which belong together, respond radically differently: the Chinese choose the cow and the grass 'because the cow eats grass'; the Europeans the hen and the cow 'as they are both animals'.

The focus on relationships as the conduit through which business is transacted leads to a form of capital being built up which is immensely valuable. It's called *Guanxi*, a complex networking web of relationships built up over time, where the network participants all trust each other and regularly confer benefit on each other in the expectation of reciprocation in due course. Such *guanxi* takes time to build, which is why successful foreign operators in China have one thing in common – they live there or spend considerable parts of their time there. Relationships cannot be built in the time intervals allowed by hectic travel schedules. They are the result of many interactions, many meals composed of strange foods, many *baijou* (Chinese *poitín*) outings, many sorry sorry mornings of post-*baijou* regret. And the necessity for such relationship-building explains why unsuccessful businesspeople get frustrated about the fact that they've 'been in China four times this year and I still don't have a contract'. The frustration is the result of an inability to do business the Chinese way, on their own terms. Like most places, you either do it their way or it doesn't get done. Don't come to

China unless you are prepared to devote the necessary time to make this kind of personal investment.

And it's really quite a clever system, you know. Why do business with people whom you aren't sure you can trust – or aren't sure how they'll react when the chips are down? *Guanxi* is really a very complex mutual testing system for human personality traits before trust can be built. Certainly, since I've been in China and learned some Chinese ways, I have adopted *guanxi* in my work in Europe. I take longer with people now to do deals until I'm sure of them. It's a system that works in the long term but takes longer to effect in the short term. Chinese businessmen often read the classic war text *The Art of War* by Sunzi (Sun Tzu). There it says 'One cannot enter alliances without knowing the designs of one's allies.' Sound advice … from 2,500 years ago.

And *guanxi* is based, at least in part, on Confucian principles, as illustrated by some of his pithy tenets:

'In his errors a man is true to type. Observe the errors and you will know the man.'

'The cautious seldom err.'

'It does not matter how slowly you go as long as you do not stop.'

All of these exhort behavioural patterns of forming relationships slowly, the better to get acquainted with potential partners, but, in the process of relationship-forming, studying the potential partner to get a better idea of how trustworthy he or she might prove.

This Confucian notion of reciprocity is responsible for the Chinese attitude towards the sacrosanct Western notion of a contract. In European thought, a contract is a definitive document that guides future business conduct within the context of the contractual subject matter area. In China, a contract is the representation at the time of signature of what each of the parties then meant. Should one party have a reason to seek a change in terms (or even contract abandonment), the parties should renegotiate so that the new contract will then better represent an equal relationship within the newly changed circumstances. Forget the notion of suing on the contract; rely instead on your relationship to try and mitigate the effect of the changes against you. To be fair to the Chinese, if your circumstances change, they will often change a contract to their own detriment to help you out.

Further Chinese business behavioural patterns are derived from one of the deepest of Confucius's teachings: the superiority of exemplification over explicit rules of behaviour. This results in indirectness in dealings with the Chinese, where more is unsaid than said and what is happening is picked up from context rather than speech. Rare is the encounter where Chinese explicitly state what they want and, often, objectives are couched in a type of mysticality, never directly saying what they think. In such encounters, it pays to *Listen, Listen, Listen*. This gives you the time to reflect on what they're trying to impart and avoids a typical Western response of jumping in feet first and suggesting a solution to what it is you think you've heard them say is their problem. Wait a little longer and you'll get the sniff of what the problem really is – as greater time in letting them speak results in more and more of the wrapping around the problem being torn away and the real one exposed. Then, but only then, ought you to offer your precious Western solution.

Failure to pierce the Chinese Veil of Thinking results in a predictable result. Back home on the plane with zero. The experience of Lord Macartney is salutary. The negotiations between him and the mandarins representing the emperor became a prolonged dance. At one banquet after another, Macartney demanded to see the emperor to present his gifts and to request greater access to China's markets. The mandarins praised the gifts and explained it would take time to set up a meeting with the emperor. Diaries and letters from both sides reveal startlingly different perceptions of what happened at these banquets. Macartney and his subordinates would congratulate themselves on having won the mandarins' confidence and prepare to depart for Beijing. The mandarins would send reports to the emperor explaining how they had massaged the barbarians' egos, while placing barriers in their way.

So, how to pierce that veil?

1. Show respect – be tough, but never show a lack of respect.

2. Expect less than reciprocation in that regard towards yourself. Chinese can be what we interpret as cruel in business relationships. The expectation that you will be sensitive to Chinese feelings and avoid one-sidedness is often an expectation of your behaviour towards them, not theirs towards you.

3. Expect lopsided proposals said with an extremely straight face. 'Blush' is not a word you would associate with Chinese businessmen.

4. As outcomes are more important than absolute truth for the Chinese, expect a cocoon to be spun of how you need them more than they need you.

5. Define your Entry Strategy, but don't stick to it. Success in China means being flexible and adapting yourself to their conditions.

6. Never say *no*. Leave open perpetual possibilities. Avoid confrontational dialogue.

7. Do *not* under any circumstances try and get a result which will result in a loss of face for your counterpart. That is a guaranteed non-happener, whatever your precious contract may say.

8. Rely more on intuitive thinking than linear analytical thinking to get what you want.

9. Never show impatience. Come with an open return ticket. The Chinese won't be rushed and impatience will be seized on as a sign of weakness.

10. Stress your long-term commitment to China and your dedication to seeing both parties benefit from the partnership. Clarify the value of your own contribution, while acknowledging and emphasising the value contributed by the Chinese partner.

11. Staff up an office that shows this long-term commitment, even if you haven't won any business.

12. Send your best people, not Joe in the office who is presently free.

Do *not* expect that this will be easy. The barriers to entry are high – language and cultural differences; almost zero protection of intellectual property; difficulties in finding the right partner; inadequate market data; the necessity of a long-term approach; protectionist tendency for domestic firms; only gradual WTO accession practices in reality; opaque, inconsistent and often arbitrary legal and regulatory systems; significant regional differences in practice, regulation, interpretation and approach. (I have not mentioned the Chinese predilection of keeping the goodies for themselves, as that practice is consistently found in nations such as USA, Canada, Mexico, Spain, France, Germany, UK and Ireland – why would you expect the Chinese to be different?)

And what if you succeed in piercing this veil? Great riches await, just as they did for those who were successful in years past, like Marco Polo, returning as a hero to Venice laden with silk and spice. The size and scale of the opportunity is unprecedented and entry now is a way to share in China's growth, establishing yourself as a favoured 'old hand' partner. The imbalances endemic in the Chinese economy *will* be ironed out by its ultra-smart government, with an inevitable strengthening of domestic demand unleashing China's enormous savings ratio of 50 per cent

China *and the* Irish

(Ireland's is c.15 per cent; UK 6 per cent; US near zero) to explode consumption of goods by an avaricious market-driven consumer.

So how, I hear you ask, can you get in on this far distant land of strange habits and customs? You may be surprised to hear that you have a comparative advantage being Irish. Why is that? We pose no threat to China, having consistently supported its position in the UN. We are not a colonial nation, having ourselves once been colonised. So we don't bring along the same baggage as those ex-imperialists such as the UK, Germany, France, the US and Japan, all of whom have hideously mistreated China in years past. China admires us as a small nation that had almost zero natural resources, an island nation cut off from Europe at its periphery, which somehow fought its way up, punching well beyond its natural weight. They see ours as a land of artists and musicians and the country that has produced the most Nobel Laureates in literature. Among those who are aware of where Ireland is, there is admiration. And the further comparative advantage in being Irish is the availability to you, to aid your endeavour, of Ireland's incredibly strong and commercially driven diplomatic force in China. Here are personnel of the very first rank in international quality and I am forever grateful for all the help afforded us by the elegantly learned and highly effective Ambassador Kelleher and Consul O'Brien in Shanghai. They, their contacts at the highest ranks of Chinese government and their intimate knowledge of China and its ways are available to any of you who care to make the journey to China. Businessmen from other nations will not find themselves blessed with a similar resource, who make themselves available so freely.

And what can you get in on? Almost everything is the answer. This is a country of 1500 cities by 2020 that is currently building 23 per annum (with 100 >1m people); a country where Shanghai increases in population every year by more than the current size of Dublin; where 50 people are worth >$1 billion; 2,000 are worth >$100m; 35,000 are worth >$10m; 150,000 are worth >$5m; 2m earn >$50,000 p.a.; where the number of buildings being erected is greater than the combined total of the rest of the world; where a starved and repressed people are being transformed into a nation of entrepreneurs and are unleashing their spending power on goods and services. In a society undergoing such rapid transformation, supplies of everything are needed, both physical goods and intellectual services.

Think about supplying what you supply at home. If they use it in Ireland, they can use it in China. You just have to make a decision to get in on the planet's biggest act; get out of your personal comfort zone and make a decision to go to China, to be part of the miracle that is China now. Come and join us and Bord Bainne and CRH and Glen Dimplex and Denis O'Brien. China has telescoped into one generation what other countries took centuries to achieve and is accomplishing two transitions at once: from a rural to an urban economy and from a command to a market one. Be witness to the world's greatest metamorphosis.

China is truly a pearl; come open its oyster.

.10.

Urban Planning in China:

Mega-cities and Beyond

PAULINE BYRNE

In China, the scale and consequences of urbanisation are profoundly different from anywhere else in the world. This is largely due to the size of its population. China's urban population, at over 540 million, is more than the total population of the enlarged EU (approximately 490 million).[1] This population is currently dispersed over 661 big, medium and small cities, of which more than 100 propose to build themselves into internationalised metropolises or mega-cities.[2] Over the next 20 years, China's urban population is predicted to grow by more than 300 million people, thus rapidly attaining urban concentration rates of more developed countries. To imagine this, picture the entire population of the United States on the move to cities!

What is at stake here is not merely the fact of social change but the speed with which it is happening. In effect, China will complete in just a few decades the urbanisation process which took Western developed countries three to four hundred years – the transformation from an agricultural society to an industrialised society, and beyond that to a services economy.

In this essay I would like to examine the strategies adopted by Central Government and some of the major Chinese cities to focus urbanisation and economic development. In doing so, I wish to emphasise the astonishing achievements of the Chinese government in directing and facilitating urban growth. But we must understand where and how these policies are now reaching their limits. In closing, I would like to consider what the current situation will teach us about the future for China which now, in a newly globalised world, will also involve the future for us here in the West.

✯

Under communism, China has operated in the context of long-term centralised planning. In theory, this still holds true for urban planning. For instance, currently in China, the same urban planning and design standards apply throughout the country – whether in the most northeasterly and coldest provincial capital of Harbin or the tropical cities of Guangxi in the south: thus carried out with minimum consideration of climate, local topography or customs. This centralised planning is applied to a land mass similar to that of the United States. The government's sense of its role is exemplified by how it handles time zones: in China, the entire country belongs to the same time zone as Beijing, whereas the USA has four time zones.

What are the consequences of this style of planning when applied to issues of urban development?

Let us look, for instance, at the recent history of China's regional development. In the move toward a full market economy which began back in 1978 with Deng Xiaoping's Reform and Opening Up policy, China established Special Economic Zones. These Special Economic Zones, centrally implemented, gave rise to huge economic success and consequent rapid urban growth in cities such as Shenzhen, Guangzhou (Canton) and Shanghai, setting models for economic and urban growth elsewhere within China.

Since the 1990s the government has been seeking to redirect targeted growth and development by a further series of regional plans which eases the pressure on the eastern half of the country, where 94 per cent of the country's population is located.

The aim is to narrow the economic gap between regions, foster balanced regional development and ease emerging social conflict. The two principal policies of regionalisation are the *Go West* policy, which was initiated in the late 1990s with a focus on Sichuan Province in the south-west of the country, and then the 2003 plan to *Revitalise the North-east*, its old industrial base, centred on Shenyang and Harbin. In addition to these two main policies, in March 2004, the *Rise of Central China* strategy was implemented to address six of central China's poorest provinces.

Despite such vigorous regionalisation policies, as the market economy mechanism has grown in importance, it is becoming more and more difficult for Central Government to direct the economy itself and the level of urbanisation that ensues from its development. For instance, prior to the economic reforms of 1978, the Chinese government was able to shape urban development through population mobility control. Through a household registration system called *hukou*, it was able to limit unauthorised migration from the countryside to cities, such as the massive migration of the peasants of Anhui to the building sites of Beijing.

However, since 1978, the Chinese government's influence on urban development has been diminishing. This is largely due to the intensification of market forces which the government itself has set in motion. In effect the economic boom of the past 20 years, focused on the main urban centres, has led to the relaxation of the *hukou* system, allowing more people to move, work and live almost anywhere in the country – albeit with lesser rights than the natives of any given location. This has had the result of accelerating the depopulation of rural areas and

plunging some of these even deeper into poverty and despera-
tion, while at the same time accelerating the growth of cities
throughout the country.

✶

In the old economic plans from Central Government – before
the introduction of the market economy in 1978 – goals and
strategies for each city were established by the central planning
commission. Cities then had very little say in how they saw their
area developing. However, today each city creates its own strategy
and vision for the future. Consequently, Chinese urban areas must
plan their own development within an environment of intense
competition, now also involving domestic rivalry with other
Chinese cities, in addition to competing at the international level.
So how do the developments in Shanghai and Beijing serve as
examples of what Chinese cities are doing to attract investment
to their own regions?

One answer is that of 'theming towns'. Today the West is fashionable in China. The country as a whole is experiencing a major
rollout of themed developments in the suburbs of its principal
cities, attempting to lure the emerging middle class with the
promise of a Western lifestyle. For instance, as around Shanghai,
some are themed in Disney-like fashion as European countries –
Thamestown, Dutch Town, German Town, Italian Town. **[figure
19]** The attributes of these towns often bear little resemblance to
their namesakes – but play on some contrived image of, for
example, German modernism, or of English villages, down to 'ye
olde village pub'! Although the very idea is enough to make a
Westerner wince, these new themed developments typically sell
very well – the more alluring the image, the better. However,
they are often underpopulated as their owners purchase these
villas as investments, leaving them more like ghost-towns.

Clearly 'realism' or even realistic expectations have little to do
with this kind of consumer-branded development. Added to this
are the unrealistic aspirations of many other new developments.
Take, for example, those going forward in areas of the country
with severe water shortages, such as in and around Beijing.

117

China *and the* Irish

Though living with a predominantly desert climate, Beijing is seeing the development of new residential areas such as the Yosemite Villa Development, where hot spring water is pumped into every villa. While this might be old news in Las Vegas or Dubai, the simple fact is that, given the population growth and development pressures on water provision, local and national government cannot afford to accommodate these whims of the newly wealthy or perceived demands of foreign nationals.

Another response is city specialisation. A more market-responsive and perhaps industrious approach to new town development is manifest in the strategic approach to creating new towns centred around selected industries.

To relieve the city from housing pressure due to staggering population growth, Shanghai Government Policy has directed the growth of three major towns around Shanghai (Jiading-Anting, Songjiang, Lingang) each specialising in key areas of the economy, plus a series of smaller towns.

For example, Lingang New Port City will emerge as a new city of 800,000 people at the easternmost tip of the Shanghai region, close to Shanghai's new deepwater port – Yangshan. Lingang, designed by German architects GMP, is physically defined by a large manmade lake in the centre of the city, called Water Drop Lake. The lake is used by Lingang in all marketing material as a unique selling point on a way of life, on quality of living and an aspiration to a lifestyle focused on leisure over hard work. Despite this marketing theme, one local government official remarked – convincingly – that 'the Chinese will never learn the Western concept of leisure'.

In addition, new eco-cities are being developed which might just lead the way toward sustainable city building, not just in China but worldwide, to tackle the environmental impacts of urbanisation. Dongtan on Chongming Island in the mouth of the Yangtze (just north of Shanghai) is being developed as a new living environment incorporating the best of an environmentally friendly development. **[see cover image and figure 20]** Located at the edge of Shanghai, in the short term it will attract the very wealthy able to afford the luxury of protecting the environment. In the longer term, this town may become a prototype for a way of building new communities, but ones affordable to the ordinary folk.

✷

Another way of attracting investment is to enhance city competitiveness. Shanghai, for instance, will continue to be a central instance of China's new urbanisation as it redefines itself to accommodate a population (by 2020) of 20 million (from current 18 million+).[3] **[figure 21]**

In the not so distant past, Shanghai was synonymous with industry and production which capitalised on its role as a major port. Like many cities worldwide that have passed through the industrialisation process, Shanghai has now become too expensive for manufacturing. As industry pulls out looking for cheaper land and labour, Shanghai is seeking to consolidate its position as an international centre for trade, to add value to its profile and to compete internationally as a global city. In the space of 25 years, the city has built 6,000 skyscrapers.[4] It is rapidly evolving from a city based on primary and secondary industries to one focusing on the tertiary and services sector. A new city strategy defines six key areas for economic development to consolidate Shanghai as a global city in the mindset of the world.

A witness to this is the growth of Pudong, across the Huangpu River from the historic centre of Shanghai. Over the past 20 years, it has emerged from swampland and warehousing to become the international financial centre of China, with the country's tallest buildings.

In addition, Shanghai is remarkable among large Chinese cities in recognising the value of conserving its historic city in terms of tourism and the value of place-making in attracting international investment. The turn-of-the-century villa houses of the French Concession district have now become home to many foreign embassies and international executives commanding top salaries. This initiative includes Xintiandi, a reconstruction of an historic city quarter in central Shanghai. It has become successful as a destination for upmarket boutiques, Starbucks and other international brands, appealing in particular to the international community and moneyed Chinese classes. So successful is Xintiandi (similar to the popularity of Dublin's Temple Bar) that this formula is being replicated across other Chinese cities from Chongqing to Wuhan.[5] Again the question arises as to the authenticity of replicated formulas. When a successful formula is recreated time and again across China, it becomes meaningless, with no roots in the local environment.

✫

These cities are competing with each other but also with comparable cities around the world. To enhance their competitiveness, both national and local planning authorities make conscious use of staging major events to raise the profile of China's cities as players on the world stage. Such events provide the opportunity to showcase this 'open economy with special Chinese characteristics', as the current market reforms are called. They also provide the impetus for Central Government to exploit the global marketing profile of these cities. In doing so, they seek to encourage sustainable development, tackling environmental problems which, if left unchecked, could ultimately hinder aspirations of China becoming a world tourist destination. The state of air pollution in Beijing is an obvious example.

The organisers for the Beijing Olympics promised a 'Green' Olympics. However, Beijing is now one of the world's dirtiest cities, with air pollution levels often two or three times the maximum allowed by the WHO. Many heavy industries and power plants were moved out of the city in preparation for the games – and much of the city's industry was shut down during the Olympics. Beijing organisers promised the International Olympic Committee to close factories and take one-third of the city's 3 million cars off the roads for the three weeks of the games in August 2008, leaving relatively clear blue skies over Beijing for the Olympics.[6] These measures once again beg the question of what will happen over the long term to such initiatives *after* the Olympics? In other words, how sustainable *are* the developments associated with China's mega-cities? London, the 2012 Olympic

City, has, for example, established the Olympic Legacy Directorate to develop a framework for a sustainable reuse of the East London games site after 2012.[7]

The Beijing Olympics in 2008 is only one instance of a major Chinese city drawing global media attention. The sheer range of events taking place in China illustrates the aggressive nature with which the country is seeking to establish itself on the world stage, as an economic power as well as a world player. These include: the Shanghai World Expo and the Asian Games in Guangzhou (Canton) (both planned for 2010), Shanghai's new Formula 1 Stadium, as well as inclusion of China on the world golf and tennis circuits – along with other sports. All this in the face of stiff competition from more developed countries, such as Ireland, which may feel that they are losing their competitive edge.

In all this frenzied drive for economic and urban development, the fundamental issues of the environment, social development and people are sometimes put to one side. Cities are about people. What is happening in China should serve as a reminder to Ireland. In Chinese urban planning, people are either not considered or there is a belief that these issues can be managed in time.

Maybe so. Maybe not.

It is evident worldwide that, in the process of economic growth, a certain level of development first has to be achieved before the higher values of environmental protection and human welfare are considered. Who will worry about the long-term hazards of air pollution if they don't know whether they can afford to feed their family next month?

There are also lessons to be learned in the mass relocation and rehousing of people, often moved from inner-city neighbourhoods to estates on the periphery of China's major urban areas. In this relocation, many have been provided for the first time with running water, indoor sanitation facilities and their own kitchens. On the other hand, these people have lost the integrity of their former neighbourhoods, both in terms of their own history and relationships with their own part of the city. As the Chinese family is heavily reliant on relatives, and in particular on grandparents, for rearing the next generation, the true extent of this loss may be even greater in China than in the West.

Furthermore, in China little thought has been given to the lessons learnt in the West where these massive housing areas have occasionally become social time-bombs: witness the 2007 riots in the Cités of Paris or indeed the riots of London's mass housing developments in the 1980s and 1990s.

Finally, economic development has brought, in Ireland as well as in China, large disparities of wealth. In most Chinese cities, where first and third worlds often live side by side, these can be glaring and certainly contribute to nascent social unrest. In China, these disparities are even greater over the rural-urban divide, where it is understandably hard for a peasant farmer whose annual income is less than 400 US$[8] to work in cities with thousands of BMWs and Mercedes clogging the highways. What brings these farmers to the city is the chance of benefiting from the promise of cash income. This immigration from the countryside to the cities involves a migrant workforce of some 200 million (almost equal to the combined populations of the UK, France and Germany). As such, these farmer-turned-worker migrants represent the largest population movement in China's history.[9] Their comings and goings are so transitory that population growth of large Chinese cities is hard to track. The official population of, for example, Beijing is 12 million – while unofficially it is estimated the real population could be almost 1.5 times that!

There are other overwhelming problems – but ones that might have been anticipated from the West's previous experience. Almost without fail, Chinese cities are adopting the American model of city building: that is, one based on the automobile. Even while US cities such as Boston are seeking to bury their highway mistakes underground through the city centre, immense highways are being layered through Chinese cities to cater to the huge growth in car ownership and the expansion of the city. Already more than a thousand new cars are sold *every day* in Beijing. Currently car ownership in China stands at 24 cars per 1,000 population and is forecast to rise – this is compared to 500 cars per 1,000 people in the EU.[10] Should Chinese car ownership levels approach those of the West, not only will it mean severe congestion in Chinese cities, where traffic chaos already reigns, but it will lead to overwhelming pollution issues and huge increases in the cost of oil worldwide.

Over the last twenty years, China has been experiencing what has been called 'a potted history of urbanisation'. It is a tribute to the policies of the central government that China has been successful at reducing overall poverty in the country, recognised by the United Nations in their report on 'The Millennium Development Goals'.[11] But today, urban poverty is on the rise with unemployment emerging as an acute current issue. Observers often comment that mistakes which the West has made could now be avoided. However, the government's main policy plank is to deliver 'prosperity and progress'. This insistence has been particularly loud since 1989. With such overwhelming pressure simply to grow and develop, learning from the mistakes of the West may not seem to be a priority, at least in the near and medium term – unless the cost of economic growth comes to be seen by the ordinary Chinese people as a price too high to pay.

What lies ahead for China's mega-cities? It is the large planning ideas of emerging cities that will bring about major change in China, as they grow, prosper and compete for both domestic and global finite resources and investment. While media coverage of China principally focuses on the country's eastern seaboard as the driver of the economy, the country's growing urban centres further afield are each seeking to stake a claim in this drive for development. Striving to distinguish themselves both domestically and at the international level, to rise above the 'made in China' branding and to be world cities in their own right, these cities will continue to compete internally, and internationally, for investment.

China *and the* Irish

In the drive for economic success in the Special Economic Zones of former times, the challenge of growth has often overlooked the fundamentals of sustainable development. In the emerging secondary cities, the nature of the challenge has changed. The economic and political context has broadened and competition has intensified such that sustainable development will be essential to ensure a competitive edge over the long term.

In conclusion, the statistics relating to urban development in China are astounding – and for the West, ultimately incomprehensible, as they almost defy comparison at a scale that we can relate to. The intensity of China's development dwarfs that of much of the world[12] – in city building and in infrastructure provision from housing to ports and airports, to road-rail-bridge infrastructure, to telecommunications and to industrial infrastructure.

Yet China can learn much from the past mistakes and the successes of Western and international city building, and in so doing avoid environmental and social problems down the line. But this might no longer be a matter of choice. One of the lessons to be learned from China's rapid urbanisation process is that at some point governments may lose control to the sheer forces of economic development itself. What is actually occurring in terms of Chinese urban growth leaves open the question as to how much can be directed – and how much will simply happen as the result of the market forces originally unleashed by the central government in 1978.

It is clear, however, that the cities that manage to capitalise on their inherent strengths – including people, place and natural assets – are those that will become the most successful over the long term. But cities are not static. They constantly need to reinvent and redefine their roles at both national and global levels.

Perhaps this is where the West will learn from China. Due to the scale and speed of city-building there, China may well have to evolve new solutions for environmental protection more rapidly than the West, due to the sheer pressure on the country's eco-system. For example: new models in planning and building cities, urban transportation and energy production could be fostered here which will allow China to continue its extraordinary economic growth while protecting its future survival. Something the West is still struggling to come to terms with.

Fundamentally, the rules of city building still apply in China, as everywhere. Cities are about people. If people are forgotten in the drive to create a global image or a competitive profile, then ultimately the city will fail and social problems will emerge that, to put right retrospectively, will cost dearly.

As cities in the West are now learning, and to their ongoing cost.

.11.

China Comes to Ireland

✶

RUADHÁN MAC CORMAIC

In 'The Sisters', the opening story in Joyce's *Dubliners*, the young narrator makes his way along Great Britain Street, north of the Liffey, to the home of his recently deceased mentor, Father Flynn. He comes upon the little house adjoining a drapery shop and finds a crape bouquet tied to the door-knocker and a card pinned to the door, announcing the man's death.

He then turns and walks slowly down Great Britain Street, reading the theatrical advertisements in the shop windows as he goes. As he walks he tries to remember the dream he had last night, after first hearing of Father Flynn's passing. He remembers long velvet curtains and a swinging lamp of antique fashion. He remembers feeling he had been very far away, in the East somewhere, in a land where the customs were strange.

'The Sisters' is a story about paralysis; Joyce's subject matter the Catholic *petit bourgeois* of *fin de siècle* Dublin and the confined spaces in which they moved. Father Flynn, having suffered a stroke, is quite literally a victim of paralysis; but so too, in another sense, is Great Britain Street, site of the young boy's reverie and then his imagined escape to the idealised, exotic East.

The Great Britain Street on which Joyce's narrator saw fit to muse on paralysis and an unlikely escape to the East is today's Parnell Street, one of modern Dublin's flag-carriers for resurgence and renewal and the one street where, most visibly, the East has come to Dublin.

Today, the casual walker on Parnell Street finds himself in an incipient Chinatown, where the visitor from Beijing or Chengdu can easily immerse herself in the rhythms and accents of home. One passes not theatrical advertisements but the menus of Sichuanese restaurants, Chinese hairdressers, mobile phone shops, internet cafés and delis. Around the corner on Mao Jie, as Moore Street is known to the city's Chinese, one can pick up Chinese editions of *Cosmo* and *Vogue* or one of three Chinese newspapers published in the city, each one containing advertisements for outposts of the vast commercial edifice that has been built around the new community: travel agencies, insurance companies or some of the 300 Chinese restaurants now operating in the greater Dublin area.

In a sense, that nexus of inner-city streets symbolises the larger changes wrought during a decade of rapid immigration into Ireland. People from more than 150 countries have settled here in recent years, and a nation of notorious monoglots now encompasses almost 170 languages. Their presence has brought a range of new religions, cultures and experiences into the frame of a relatively homogenous society, turning one of Europe's leading exporters of youth into one of its most cosmopolitan magnet-states.

And just as Ireland's rehearsal of the migration debate is being played out on the fringes of a larger, planetary drama, the influx of Chinese to Ireland is also part of something greater.

Migration is not new to China, and in one sense Ireland's Chinese are re-enacting a long-standing tradition. Traders and Buddhist pilgrims reached the shores of Southeast Asia and India centuries before Western explorers. As Frank Pieke demonstrates, China – like so many modern states – owes some of its shape and complexion to people's tendency to move from one place to another. 'After all, military conquest, trade and migration generally accompanied the expansion of the Chinese empire and the sinification of the peoples that came under its control. The Chinese Communist Party, too, uses migration of the majority Han-Chinese ethnic group to strengthen its grip over territories such as Tibet and Xinjiang chiefly inhabited by non-Han peoples,' he writes.[1]

Yet the current surge in Chinese migration is more than a renewal of past trends. The number of people involved, the swiftness with which it took off and the inability of the authorities to control it make migration a child of the new prosperous and dynamic society that has emerged in China in recent decades.[2]

In Ireland, the Chinese have been an established – albeit modestly sized – immigrant group for decades. The so-called 'settled' Chinese are those Cantonese-speakers who came from Hong Kong via Britain since the 1950s, at a time when many of their compatriots were drawn by the potential of the catering trade across post-war Europe. In Northern Ireland, Hong Kongers came in even greater numbers from the 1960s; they have remained one of the largest minority ethnic groups there ever since. In the 1970s the numbers of Chinese increased with the arrival of students from Malaysia, Singapore and Taiwan and by some immigrant professional workers. But this contingent – largely Cantonese-speakers – are thought to have numbered only a few thousand, most of them settling in Dublin.

In the 1990s, with China's progressive integration into the world's economy, the profile of its émigrés shifted again. Under the new order, remittances from old emigrants became less important as international exchanges in the high-technology sectors and the expansion of Chinese firms' international markets became a new priority.[3] And on this newly configured stage, students were to have a leading role.

Until the late 1970s China's few student exchange programmes were mostly with the Soviet Union. But from the end of that decade, at the initial urging of Deng Xiaoping, the spectrum of possibility for the aspirant young widened exponentially, and in the past 15 years support for overseas study has become a plank of China's national development strategy.

As a result, Chinese student numbers have risen rapidly across Europe – and young students from mainland China now form by far the largest group of Chinese in Ireland. Their path was cleared first by official inducement – for example, a government decision in 2000 to allow all non-European students to work part-time to help finance their studies – and, second, by the intensive efforts of those Irish universities and private language schools that saw in China's burgeoning and mobile middle class a lucrative and apparently inexhaustible source of income.

Across China, hundreds of Western education agencies vie with one another to lure abroad the sons and daughters of the boom. Dublin Business School, which has for years been courting Chinese applicants, now has 22 agents recruiting prospective students in China, including nine in Beijing, five in Shanghai, two in Dalian and one in Chengdu. The result of such efforts is that in some Dublin language schools there are classrooms composed entirely of Chinese students. And though their numbers are smaller, the universities, which stand to gain three times more in fees from a Chinese student than they do from an Irish one, have enthusiastically followed suit. According to the last census, there were just over 11,000 Chinese living in the Republic in April 2006, almost twice the number reported four years earlier – and enough to make them the seventh largest immigrant group in the state. Many, including the government and the Chinese embassy, believe the figure could be higher. They are overwhelmingly young, single and urban.[4]

Chinese migrants to Europe traditionally came from the southern coastal provinces adjacent to Hong Kong and Taiwan, but many now come to Europe from the major cities and from the so-called 'rust belt' in the north-east of the country. A report by Lan Li and Richard O'Leary showed that most Chinese language students in Ireland came from the same two provinces: the majority (60 per cent) originated in Liaoning in the northeast, while the next most popular source province was Fujian in the south, home to 15 per cent of them. Almost 90 per cent came from urban China. And compared to their peers at home, these language-school students were highly educated – almost half had degrees from China; the other half were educated to secondary level.[5]

The title of a recent academic paper on the ethnic Chinese in Ireland – 'Celtic Tiger, Hidden Dragon'[6] – makes reference to the popular perception that Ireland's Chinese live at a certain remove, that their remarkable integration into the economy has never been matched by their incorporation into society. Integration, of course, is a nebulous, problematic term. But according to the findings of a recent large-scale study carried out by researchers at UCD for the Immigrant Council of Ireland, there might be something in the assumption.

From their assessment of the integration of four migrant groups (Lithuanians, Chinese, Indians and Nigerians) using a selection of political, economic, social and cultural indicators, intriguing patterns arose. First, the Chinese show unusually low rates of participation in political activities and in trade unions.[7] Of the four groups, the Chinese were more likely to regularly spend time with Irish people but not necessarily more likely to form a close bond with them. They had a strong desire for social inter-action with Irish people, but the desire was thwarted by pressure on people's lives, the language barrier, limited spaces for social interaction and the perceived difficulties of forming close friend-ships with the Irish.

One university student, quoted by Li and O'Leary, speaks for many when he says: 'Even with some close friends the conversa-tion has never gone very deep. It is always very shallow and not like the conversation I had with my friends in China.'[8]

On the surface, the Chinese have something of an advantage over other migrant groups: many are students with Irish class-mates, and at work most of them deal with Irish colleagues and customers every day. But over four-fifths (84.3 per cent) say that they live with only Chinese housemates and an almost identical proportion (83 per cent) report that all their friends are Chinese.[9]

Because they need to study to retain their visa and then to work to sustain themselves, there is little time left for much else. One student remarked that a social life could be construed in different ways. 'For me the definition of social life is to enjoy when you are working because you spend about 30/40 hours per week. So, if you can enjoy that, that's your social life.'[10]

A 40-year-old salesperson quoted elsewhere believes that the role in which Ireland's Chinese are cast is also a significant hindrance to their participation. 'I cannot integrate into the Irish society,' he says. 'I am always the worker who works for the Irish.'[11]

If we can only tentatively explore the connections between Chinese and Irish, the same is true of another relationship: that is, how Chinese immigrants relate to one another. By one gauge, at least, we find divergent trends on either side of the border.

In Northern Ireland, the long-established Chinese Welfare Association is a large advocacy group originally set up by Cantonese speakers from Hong Kong. It was once chaired by Anna Lo, who in 2007 became the first minority ethnic candidate to be elected to the Stormont Assembly. A second organisation, the Mandarin Speakers' Association, fulfils a similar function, providing classes, social events and guidance to mainland Chinese émigrés.

But in the Republic of Ireland, where other large migrant groups have established sophisticated networks of representation and association, it appears the Chinese have been slower to form themselves into groups. In general one finds less cohesion, and where Chinese groups do exist, they tend to be small, loosely focused ones catering for particular – often sub-national – groups. The Chinese Professionals' Association represents the interests of Hong Kong businessmen, for instance, and there are a number of groups that bring together migrants from Fujian province. The Chinese Information Centre was established after the murder of a young Chinese immigrant who died after being struck in the head with an iron bar by a gang of teenagers in Dublin in 2002. It offers advice and support to young people who run into trouble. But such bodies are small, poorly funded and limited in their reach. There is no association for language-school students, although they form the majority of the Chinese population.

This fragmentation is perceived by the Chinese themselves. Only half of respondents in one study agreed that there was such a thing as a Chinese community in Ireland. When those who believed there was such a thing were asked if they felt they belonged to that community, only a third said they did.[12]

One explanation may be that so many students regard their sojourn in Ireland as just that – a temporary stopover en route to an elevated perch on the career ladder back home.

Dr Liming Wang, director of UCD's Confucius Institute, has been a migrant on both sides of the border, having spent more than 15 years in Belfast before moving to Dublin two years ago. He suggests that, as a minority ethnic group in a society as polarised as Northern Ireland's, the Chinese had more of a need to seek one another out, whereas in the arguably more benign environment of the south, there was not the same need to coalesce.[13]

That is not to say that the Chinese migrant's experience of the Republic is without its difficulties. In fact, the picture presented by recent research suggests that for the Chinese student-workers the experience is bleaker than for many others.

According to one study of four migrant groups, it was the Chinese who experienced the broadest range of problems at work. They also reported the lowest levels of income – 59 per cent said their average annual income was less than €14,400.[14]

Researchers also find consistently high levels of anxiety among Chinese students about their immigration status, and since an official tightening of visa regulations in 2005, some have fallen on the wrong side of the law but continue to work without valid papers. Losing their status creates in turn new difficulties, leaving them more exposed to discrimination and, when in difficulties, less likely to contact the Gardaí (the Irish police), public bodies or the churches.

Even among those who study English, many feel they make little progress with the language. One student suggested why that might be. 'Many [language] students, especially those from Fujian province, have borrowed a lot of money to come to Ireland. Usually their parents borrowed about 130,000 yuan [about €13,000] and gave this money to agencies for getting everything done for their children going abroad. After these students arrived at Ireland, therefore, the first thing for them to do was not to learn English but to clear the debt. They work extremely hard and share a room with five or six people. ... In this situation they simply don't have any time for study. ... Plus they shared [a] room with their countrymen and always spoke local dialect to each other. So they had little chance to practise English at home.'[15]

Money – or the lack of it – is the concern around which all others turn. Dr Lan Li of UCD says most young Chinese mainlanders come to Ireland with the intention of eventually going to university; but very quickly they realise it's an impossible hope. She calculates that if a Chinese student worked full-time for a year, keeping living expenses to a minimum, all his/her savings would probably not support one year at an Irish university, where tuition fees for foreign students can amount to €15,000 a year.[16]

One 26-year-old language student described the sort of routine that would be familiar to many of her compatriots. 'I worked seven days a week for two years. During the week, I had to wake up at 5am and started work at 6. From 6 to 7am I cleaned the casino. Then I cleaned a big pub, which included a restaurant as well. I finished that work at noon. Then from 12.30 to 2.30pm I cleaned an office. After that I went home to have a break. Then from 4 to 6pm I worked in an office. Usually I could finish before 6. From 6pm to 10pm I studied in the language school.'[17]

When things don't work out, simply returning home is not always seen as an option. Often, extended families will have pooled their money for the only child's trip to Ireland. A sense of shame prevents them from returning home empty-handed, particularly if they have not told their parents the truth about their experience here.

And what of racism? We know that most Chinese student-workers claim to have experienced some form of racial discrimination, and anecdotes about casual insults, taunts and physical attack are common among the Chinese. But despite being disproportionately affected by crime, the Chinese are among the least likely to report their experiences to the Gardaí. When I asked one Chinese migrant why that might be, she reminded me that the Chinese symbol for government is composed of two mouths under a roof. 'An ordinary person has one mouth, the government has two,' she said. 'Who wins? People don't want anything to do with government. The government is for imposing the law, not for helping us.'

Problems are compounded by a general lack of knowledge about rights and redress. One language student tells of how he and a compatriot kept two cats in the flat they rented when they first came to Ireland, but when their landlord discovered the cats, he threw the students out, leaving them at a loss as to what they could do. 'We became homeless and walked about in the street. We spent two nights in an internet café, one night in the airport and one night in a hotel with a cost of €120.'[18]

Inevitably, the cumulative effect of these pressures is a feeling of social isolation, a recurrent theme in conversations with Chinese students. 'Remember that Chinese are one-child families. Emotionally, they're very dependent,' says Katherine Chan-Mullen, founder of the Chinese Information Centre. 'It's the culture. The students are so dependent, emotionally they're very weak. They come here and they're lonely. The first problem is not the money gap, it's that they must learn to be independent, to be strong internally.'[19]

Since the 1970s, it has been Communist Party policy to encourage the 'overseas Chinese' to return home one day. And in Ireland too, official fostering of the migration route between the two countries has been founded on the assumption that China's student visitors will be just that. The state gains by receiving diligent workers to fill the service jobs that Irish people spurn as well as students who pay full university fees. It is also aware that it does no harm to relations with the Chinese behemoth to have so many of its young people educated here. But is it right to assume that their stay is temporary?

The international record suggests that, on completion of their studies overseas, the majority of Chinese students choose not to return home. Generally, they take up employment in the destination country, continue further studies or move to somewhere else.[20] It is perhaps too early to say where the paths that have brought so many Chinese students to Ireland will eventually lead, and their future decisions, one can assume, will reflect the internal diversity of the group. Many will have prospered with their time abroad, but it is evident also that there are others who will have reluctantly abandoned their original plans and whose ambitions have been tempered by their lives abroad.

For the minority who have studied at university and who will probably have the funds and the qualifications, new horizons beckon. But this won't be true of thousands of language-school students who have found themselves locked into a cycle of perpetual low-wage service jobs; for these, the dream of a university place grows dimmer by the week.

There are, of course, those who want to stay. Frank Heran Suo, a 25-year-old student, likens the overseas Chinese to the Jews of the nineteenth century and says most harbour the hope of returning home one day. But Frank has been living here since he was 18 – and after seven years, he admits to having grown accustomed to the Irish way of life. 'When I go back to China, I don't feel I belong,' he says. 'Back in China everything is so different. The culture's different. They don't see me as a stranger but I feel like a stranger in China.'[21]

Others are ambivalent over whether to remain. 'I feel contradictory about it,' says one mother who has after many years secured her legal status in Ireland. 'My child has Irish nationality so we should educate her to get familiar with Irish life and Irish society, she should become a real Irish. However, if we stay here with her, life will be too boring for us. We don't speak English and cannot adapt to Irish society. Apart from work we keep ourselves inside all the time. We don't have any neighbours – all of our neighbours are Irish and we cannot communicate with them. So if we decide to stay, it is only for our child.'[22]

And what, then, of those who do stay? What hyphenated identities will their children grow into, and how will these new identities inform broader understandings of Irishness? A useful insight is provided by the experience of the second-generation Chinese, those Irish citizens whose parents came from Hong Kong and settled from the 1960s. Though they may value their Chinese heritage, in nearly every practical sense their experiences are those of most Irish young people, with whom they share their education, their adolescence, their mores and mannerisms. Ireland is where they belong. But, as many of them observe, there is a disjunction between their perception of themselves and the way that mainstream society regards them. Lucy, born in Ireland to Chinese parents, classes herself as Irish but finds that here there is unease with notions of hybridity, with being 'in between' – and she constantly feels herself constricted by the essentialised ethnic identity ascribed to her by others.[23] For some, the result is one of double alienation, first from one's own ethnic group and then from the society into which they anxiously seek entry.

There is always a temptation to exoticise the Chinese, fixing them in what Robin Cohen called 'some timeless and unyielding Oriental Otherness' instead of drawing their varied experiences into the common pool of human behaviour.[24] Ultimately, of course, the success of the great Sino-Irish encounter of the past decade will be measured by our capacity to avoid that temptation and to draw the Chinese experience into the ever-deepening, ever more capacious common pool that is becoming modern Ireland.

Figure 11: Birr Castle, County Offaly, Ireland: a view from the gardens.

Figure 12: *Magnolia Officinalis* in Birr Castle Gardens, as painted by Patricia Jorgenson.

Figure 13: Desmond Parsons at home in his traditional courtyard house in Peking (Beijing) during his parents' extended honeymoon to China in 1935. The figures are, from left to right: Desmond Parsons; his mother, Lady de Vesci; Anne, Countess of Rosse; and Harold Acton.

Figure 14: China's first full Ambassador to Ireland, Madame Gong Pusheng, accompanied by Dr E.C. Nelson of the Botanic Gardens, Glasnevin, on a visit to Birr Castle in 1982 with Lord Rosse and his first son, Patrick Parsons (Lord Oxmantown).

Figure 15: Baptism by Edward J. Galvin, Bishop of Hanyang (1927–56), about 1940. Courtesy of the Columban Fathers.

Figure 16: The first three Columbans to Arrive in China – Owen MacPolin, John Blowick and Edward Galvin: with Lo Pa-Hong (second from left) and family from a photograph dated 17 June 1920, the year of their arrival. The two little boys are grandchildren, Michael and Joseph. Lo Pa Hong was a businessman and an outstanding Christian. He was assassinated on 30 December 1937. Courtesy of the Columban Fathers.

Figure 17: The music programme for the Fourteenth Commencement Exercises of Peking University (10 February 1904) featuring 'the private band of Sir Robert Hart, BART'.
© Queen's University Belfast, Sir Robert Hart Collection, MS 15.

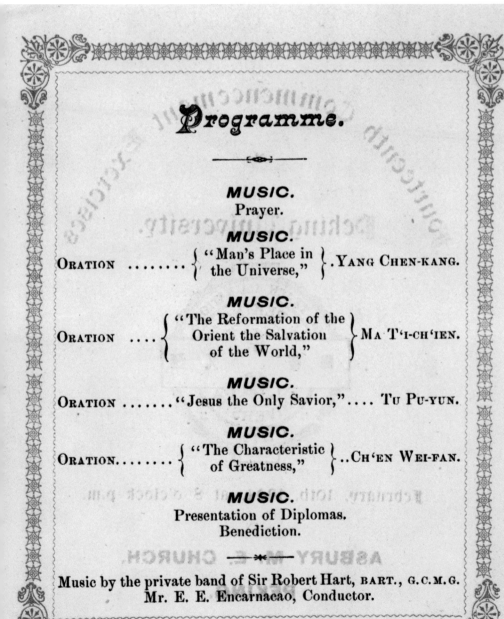

Figure 18: Robert Hart's Brass Band, under the direction of bandmaster, E.E. Encarnaçao.
© Queen's University Belfast, Sir Robert Hart Collection, MS 15.

Figure 19: Wooden Shoe, the logo for Dutch-Town, outside Shanghai.
Courtesy of Bert van Dijk, Freelance Correspondent, China.

Figure 20: The lake at Dongtan, Chongming Island.

Figure 21: Shanghai Today: one of China's fastest-growing mega-cities.

Afterword

*Marking Thirty Years of Diplomatic Relations
between Ireland and China*

DECLAN KELLEHER,
Ambassador of Ireland to China

The distinguished historian of China, Jonathan Spence, wrote that 'one aspect of a country's greatness is surely its capacity to attract and retain the attention of others'. China has never failed to attract such attention. Spence's words were focused primarily on European perceptions of China at a time when distances and travel were far more daunting than they are now, and knowledge about China was far less than it is now. China, since the days of Marco Polo, who may or indeed may not have actually reached China, has always been an object of fascination and interest.

In the thirty-one years since China launched its policy of Reform and Opening Up, which is at the heart of China's phenomenal economic and social transformation, much more international understanding of China has ensued. The success of the Beijing Olympic Games in 2008 brought modern China to the attention of the whole world.

China *and the* Irish

But it is important to recall that China's history of interaction with the wider world goes back very far indeed. Richard Barrett rightly and eloquently summarises the reality in his contribution: China is not just on the way up, China is on the way back. China accounted for a substantial proportion of world trade five hundred years ago. China's four great inventions – the compass, gunpowder, paper and printing, and its written language – are emblematic of China's development at an early stage of history. Now, China accounts for one-fifth of the population of the planet. China is a permanent member of the UN Security Council and is currently the largest contributor of personnel to UN peacekeeping operations among all of the five permanent members. China is, moreover, the third largest economy in the world and has sustained, the current economic crisis notwithstanding, extraordinarily high levels of growth year on year. The intense international interest in China's economic development and prospects, at a time of international economic recession, is further clear evidence of how China is seen in the 21st century.

China is keen to underline that it is a developing country and that it is constantly looking at new approaches in the quest to achieve its goal of economic prosperity for its people. The Chinese growth model of the last fifteen years is being adjusted to focus more on technologically sophisticated process and product and less on smokestack growth. These developments alone should be of great interest to Ireland as a trading and technologically well-endowed nation, as we seek to develop further areas for partnership with China.

A story from the classical era, entitled 瞎子摸象 (*xia zi mo xiang*), sums up the challenge of understanding a country as large and as diverse as China. It is a story about four blind men each touching an elephant, and each confidently but wrongly guessing what it is. They never reach a true understanding because they focus only on the part instead of grasping the nature of the whole. The keen-sighted contributors to this book are expert guides, focusing on different aspects of China and China/Ireland links, but also giving the reader a strong sense of China as a whole. They have combined to shed valuable light not only on history, but also on points of convergence and parallel between China and Ireland: as in, for example, the experiences of the Irish and Chinese diasporas (which are two of the largest, if not the two largest, diasporas in the world). There are also fascinating accounts of family and personal links with China which go back well before the founding of the Irish state or of our diplomatic relations. Contributions also underline that culture, whether in terms of music or literature, is an important aspect and indeed driver of our bilateral relationship; that human contacts through Chinese people living in Ireland and Irish people living in China are a valuable source of mutual understanding; that urbanisation is a common challenge and opportunity; and that, in business, building relations, familiarity and trust is the sure way to build mutual understanding, mutual respect and what the Chinese like to call a win-win solution. Increasingly, Irish entrepreneurs and companies are establishing important market presences in Beijing, Shanghai, Shenzhen and other Chinese cities.

The thirty years since diplomatic ties were established between China and Ireland have seen extraordinary economic and social developments in both countries and also the maturing of a close and friendly bilateral relationship. In recent years, that relationship has widened and deepened to encompass not only intensified political and trade relations, but also a blossoming of exchanges and relationships in third-level and postgraduate education, in food and agriculture, tourism and in new areas such as financial services and the environment and investment opportunities. Allied to these developments has been the growth of the vibrant Chinese community in Ireland and an equally vibrant Irish community in China.

This year is also the tenth anniversary of Ireland's Asia Strategy, with China at its core. The Asia Strategy, which was reviewed and relaunched in 2005, has been a useful framework to help focus Irish efforts in developing the many-dimensional relationship between our two countries. In recent years, a number of high-level visits by both sides have taken place, which nourish and give important impetus to the relationship. In addition to the visit of

China *and the* Irish

President McAleese in 2003, the previous Taoiseach Bertie Ahern TD visited China in 2005 and the current Taoiseach Brian Cowen TD visited China in 2008, each accompanied by large trade delegations. Premier Wen Jiabao and Vice Premiers Huang Ju and Zeng Peiyan have visited Ireland in recent years. Irish and Chinese Ministers have also paid and exchanged a number of visits. The success of these visits, and the growth of mutual understanding, underpin the scope for building even stronger foundations to the relationship in the coming years, in the political and the economic spheres.

As relations develop further, it will be important to keep fully in mind the potential in China as a whole, to go back to the story of the elephant. We are also raising and sustaining awareness of Ireland in China's populous inland provinces and in what are called the fast-emerging second-tier cities such as Chengdu in Sichuan province, Wuhan, Zhengzhou, Dalian and Qingdao, each of which has a population as large as, or larger than, the population of Ireland. Increasingly, Irish companies and Irish educational institutions are also building relationships in these cities and provinces.

Culture in all its forms is an important subtext of the relationship between China and Ireland. Both countries have sought to blend the traditional with the modern, not only in daily life, but also in cultural matters. Culture is, in my view, an important aspect of driving forward the political and also the trade relationship. Many countries are heavily focused on China, and it is an asset for Ireland that Chinese political and business leaders are aware of, and interested in, Ireland's achievements in literature, music and in particular *Riverdance*, which is phenomenally popular in China. It was a matter of great pride to me, to my colleagues and indeed to Irish people throughout China that *Riverdance* was chosen as the sole non-Chinese act to perform in this year's Chinese New Year TV gala show, which has enormous viewing figures.

Culture runs very deep in Chinese life. One of the most memorable, and indeed moving, days I have experienced here was late last year when I visited a primary school destroyed in the Sichuan earthquake, in follow up to the relief donation made by the Irish government and a presentation of drawings by a junior school in Ireland. The group of nine-year-old children was very well informed on Ireland and was keen to hear about the interests of Irish children. They were also keen to hear, in great detail, views about Irish perceptions of Chinese culture.

Although China and Ireland are separated by considerable geographical distance, and by size, there are parallels in historical experiences and challenges which are of interest in China and which can and do add to mutual understanding. Ireland's model of economic and social transformation over the last forty years, from an agrarian and underdeveloped country on the periphery of Europe to a high technology economy with internationally recognised strengths in software and services, and the part played in this by education and by leveraging our international influence through the European Union in particular, is of enduring interest to China as it seeks to develop its own economic and social models. There is much scope for mutually beneficial cooperation in this perspective also.

In conclusion, I commend Dr Jerusha McCormack for her tireless efforts to bring this project to reality and completion, not only as a Thomas Davis radio series, but also in the form of this book. I also congratulate RTÉ for devoting a series of the Thomas Davis lectures to China and Irish links with China. China is a subject of growing importance for all of us in Ireland. As the whole world beats a path to China, it is, I believe, very important that the richness and potential of the relationship between China and Ireland, and between Chinese and Irish people, be reflected upon. I believe that this book is a valuable step in that direction. I also believe that the book is particularly timely as 2009 marks the 30th anniversary of the establishment of diplomatic relations between Ireland and the People's Republic of China.

Notes on Contributors

✦

RICHARD BARRETT is the CEO of Treasury Holdings, the premier Irish real-estate company specialising in mixed-use sustainable development, with global interests in Ireland, the UK, Germany, Sweden, Spain, Russia and China. He holds primary and postgraduate degrees in both economics and law. He is a barrister and has been/is a director of five quoted companies, including China Real Estate Opportunities Ltd (which he founded), a London-listed company which is the largest Western real-estate company in China. Richard Barrett is also a member of the Committee for the Urban Regeneration of the City of Nanjing and was a member of the Board of Graduate School of Design at Harvard University.

PAULINE BYRNE is a Strategic Planner with Treasury Holdings. Pauline spent two years in China working on large-scale master planning and strategic planning projects that extended across the country. In addition, she has extensive experience working throughout Ireland and in the UK on a range of large-scale and complex development projects. Pauline Byrne's particular interests are in the areas of City Competitiveness and City Marketing.

THE REVD CANON PATRICK COMERFORD, B.D., Dip. Ecum., FRSAI, is Director of Spiritual Formation, Church of Ireland Theological Institute, Dublin. He is Chair and former Secretary of the Dublin University Far Eastern Mission.

DR HWEE-SAN TAN obtained her Ph.D. in ethnomusicology and completed a post-doctoral fellowship at the School of Oriental and African Studies, University of London, following a year of lecturing at University of Durham. After completing a three-year lectureship at University College, Dublin, she currently lectures at Goldsmiths College London and University of Surrey and is also a Research and Teaching Associate at SOAS. She has published several articles on Buddhist liturgical music and is currently in Fujian, China, preparing a monograph on Buddhist rites for the dead and their music.

SHANE MCCAUSLAND is Head of Collections and also Curator of the East Asian Collections at the Chester Beatty Library, Dublin. In 2003-4 he was Robert and Lisa Sainsbury Fellow in the Sainsbury Institute for the Study of Japanese Arts and Cultures, based at the School of Oriental and African Studies, University of London, where he was previously a lecturer in the Department of Art and Archaeology.

His research interests range from the history of calligraphy and painting in China to artistic ties between China and Japan. In 2003, he published *The Admonitions Scroll: First masterpiece of Chinese painting* and *Gu Kaizhi and the Admonitions Scroll* (contributing editor) (both British Museum Press), and in 2005, 'Nihonga Meets Gu Kaizhi: A Japanese copy of a Chinese painting in the British Museum', in *The Art Bulletin* (December 2005). He has recently rewritten his doctoral dissertation (Princeton, 2000) on the art of the pivotal Chinese master Zhao Mengfu (1254–1322) as a book (forthcoming from Hong Kong University Press). *Chinese Romance from a Japanese Brush – Kano Sansetsu's Chogonka Scrolls in the Chester Beatty Library* (co-authored) is forthcoming from Scala Publications in 2009. He is currently organising a major loan exhibition of figure paintings from the Shanghai Museum to be held in Dublin in 2010.

RUADHÁN MAC CORMAIC, a journalist for *The Irish Times*, won the 2008 Douglas Gageby *Irish Times* Fellowship for a project on immigration and social change in Ireland. He is a graduate of

China *and the* Irish

Trinity College, Dublin, the University of Strasbourg and Cambridge University.

JERUSHA MCCORMACK, MA and Ph.D. (Brandeis University), took early retirement after thirty years teaching in the School of English at University College, Dublin to teach in China. With research interests concentrating on the period of 1840–1920, in American, British and Anglo-Irish literature, her publications include four books on Oscar Wilde and his circle as well as articles on Emily Dickinson, American 'decadence' and Henry James. Over the last five years, she has served as Visiting Professor for the School of English and International Studies at Beijing Foreign Studies University, where she helped to found the first Irish Studies Centre in China. There she helped devise – along with Professor John Blair – a sourcebook for Chinese graduate students under the title of *Western Civilization with Chinese Comparisons* (published by Fudan University Press, 2006, in 1067 pages) now being turned around so that it can be used for students in the West. Under the title of *Comparing China and the West*, it is to be published in the US in 2011.

DR RICHARD O'LEARY, BA (UCD), D.Phil. (Oxford) is a lecturer in the School of Sociology, Queen's University, Belfast and a former Irish civil servant. He first went to China in 1987–88 as a student on the Ireland – China government exchange scholarship. He has published on minority groups in Ireland, including the Chinese, and about religion in Ireland, Europe and China. He is a co-founder and current Secretary of the Association for Chinese Studies in Ireland.

FINTAN O'TOOLE is Assistant Editor of *The Irish Times*, for whom he reported from China in 2006. His books include *Black Hole, Green Card*; *Shakespeare is Hard But So Is Life*; *Meanwhile Back at the Ranch*; *A Traitor's Kiss: The Life of Richard Brinsley Sheridan*; *White Savage: William Johnson and the invention of America*; and *The Irish Times Book of the 1916 Rising*.

SIR BRENDAN PARSONS, 7th Earl of Rosse, educated at Aiglon, the Universities of Grenoble and Oxford (MA) and with a D.LL from Dublin, spent eighteen years (from 1962–80) with the UN Development Programme in the field, serving *inter alia*, as first UN Volunteer Field Director and UNESCO Representative in Iran and UN Disaster Relief Coordinator in Bangladesh.

On his father's death, and his consequent return to Ireland to take over the heritage of Birr Castle, he was appointed to the Government's Advisory Council on Development Cooperation and to the Board of APSO (Agency of Personnel Overseas). He subsequently founded the Birr Scientific and Heritage Foundation as the vehicle to achieve, firstly, the restoration of the Great Telescope (the world's largest until a century ago) and, secondly, the creation of Ireland's Historic Science Centre. This achievement led to awards of honorary life membership of the RDS (Royal Dublin Society) and Fellowship of the IEI (Institute of Engineers of Ireland). Both a fervent nationalist and internationalist, Lord Rosse has started to change the rather fixed and outdated image of the Irish, making him an unusual force among the scions of the old Anglo-Irish aristocracy.

2. Empires at Odds: The Qianlong Emperor and Earl Macartney's British Mission
Shane McCausland

[1] For *Leabhar Ser Marco Polo (Book of Sir Marco Polo)* see the *Book of Mac Carthaigh Riabhach* (otherwise, *Book of Lismore;* compiled early fifteenth century); facsimile, ed. R.A.S. Macalister (Dublin: Stationery Office, 1950), pp. 121a1–131b2; edited by Stokes, with a translation and glossary, in *Zeitschrift für Celtische Philologie,* 1 (Halle/Göttingen 1896–8), pp. 245–73 and 362–438. The reliability of Polo's descriptions of China and of Khubilai's favour towards him have been doubted in recent years – see, e.g., Frances Wood, *Did Marco Polo Go to China?* (London: Secker & Warburg, 1995) – but his popularity as a China pioneer has not dimmed over the centuries. In 1579 Polo's account appeared in English for the first time. By the late eighteenth century, five centuries after Marco's return to Venice, it had appeared in translations in many European languages but remained one of *the* sources on China.

[2] Sources include: Helen H. Robbins, *Our First Ambassador to China: An account of the life of George, Earl of Macartney* (London: John Murray, 1908); Aubrey Singer, *The Lion and the Dragon: The story of the first British embassy to the court of the Emperor Qianlong in Peking, 1792–794* (London: Barrie and Jenkins, 1992); Blas Sierra de la Calle, *China 1793: La Embajada de Lord Macartney* (Valladolid: Museo Oriental, 2006); Robert A. Bickers (ed.), *Ritual and Diplomacy: The Macartney mission to China 1792–1794* (London: British Association for Chinese Studies, 1993).

[3] Edict from the Qianlong emperor to King George III in the collection of HM The Queen, Royal Archives, Windsor Castle. For Macartney, see Peter Roebuck (ed.), *Macartney of Lisanoure (1737–1806): Essays in biography* (Belfast: Ulster Historical Foundation, 1983), especially ch. 7 by L. Cranmer-Byng.

[4] The emperor stipulated that the actual engraved copperplates be returned to China along with the prints, although, needless to say, the engravers secretly kept copies and later reprinted them. It is possible that the emperor wanted, in this roundabout way, to crow about his achievements to the French monarch,

but more likely this stipulation owed to the emperor's obsessively secretive nature and his worries about national security.

⁵ The subject of a horizontal wall-scroll in the Palace Museum, Beijing (Gu6255), entitled *Imperial Banquet in the Garden of Ten Thousand Trees* of 1755, attributed to Castiglione and fellow Jesuits; illustrated in *China: The three emperors* (London: Royal Academy of Arts, 2005), no. 76.

⁶ It is noteworthy that in William Alexander's drawing, Macartney and his suite appear to be standing in the line of ambassadors by the tent. In later engravings based on this drawing (e.g., one by J. Fittler, London, 1796), Macartney and his attendants occupy a more elevated position in front of the line, opposite the arriving emperor; see, e.g., Singer, *The Lion and the Dragon*, pl. 9.

⁷ The phrase is borrowed from the subtitle of Joe Studwell, *The China Dream: The elusive quest for the greatest untapped market on earth* (London: Profile Books, 2003). Studwell notes (p. 10) how relations between the emerging global power of the era – the British empire – and China got off to a poor start in 1743, when George Anson, a British commodore, quarrelled with Canton authorities. Anson's ships needed repairs in port but he refused to accept a Chinese demand to pay custom duties.

⁸ Among the latter was Lord Mark Kerr, a son of the Marquis of Lothian. Some of his sketch books are in the collection of Hector McDonnell at Glenarm, Co. Antrim; Kerr's journal is kept in Glenarm Castle.

⁹ Hickey's lost portrait of Macartney as the newly ennobled Lord Macartney of Dervock (from 1792?) is the basis for an engraving by J. Hall (London, 1796). Although Hickey was the official artist to the embassy, he apparently did only a few sketches between 1792 and 1794.

¹⁰ On this topic see, e.g., J. L. Cranmer-Byng and Trevor Levere, 'A Case Study in Cultural Collision: Scientific apparatus in the Macartney embassy to China 1793,' *Annals of Science*, 38 (1981), pp. 503–25.

¹¹ For the edicts see Singer, *The Lion and the Dragon*, pl. 17 and pp. 180–6 (translated by Backhouse and Bland, *Annals and Memoirs of the Court of Peking*); Cranmer-Byng in *Macartney of Lisanoure*, esp. pp. 240–3.

3. An Irish Mandarin: Sir Robert Hart
in China 1854–1908
Richard O'Leary

¹ Katherine F. Bruner, John K. Fairbank, Richard J. Smith (eds.), *Entering China's Service: Robert Hart's journals, 1854–1863* (Cambridge, MA: Council on East Asian Studies, 1986) and Richard J. Smith, John K. Fairbank, Katherine F. Bruner (eds.), *Robert Hart and China's Early Modernization: His journals, 1863–1866* (Cambridge, MA: Council on East Asian Studies, 1991).

² Bruner et al. (1986), p. 65.

³ Hans Van de Ven, 'Robert Hart and Gustav Detring during the Boxer Rebellion', *Modern Asian Studies*, 40 (2006), 3, p. 633.

⁴ Bruner et al. (1986), p. 325.

[5] Richard Horowitz, 'Politics, Power and the Chinese Maritime Customs: The Qing Restoration and the ascent of Robert Hart,' *Modern Asian Studies*, 40 (2006), 3, p. 558.

[6] Lan Li and Deirdre Wildy, 'A New Discovery and its Significance: The statutory declarations made by Sir Robert Hart concerning his secret domestic life in nineteenth-century China', *Journal of the Hong Kong Branch of the Royal Asiatic Society* (2003), 43, p. 84.

[7] Smith et al. (1991), p. 363.

[8] Letter 473, 7 April 1884. John K. Fairbank, Katherine F. Bruner and Elizabeth Matheson (eds.), *The I.G in Peking: Letters of Robert Hart, Chinese Maritime Customs, 1868–1907*, 2 volumes (Cambridge, MA: Harvard University Press, 1975).

[9] Ibid., Letter 913, 13 December 1893.

[10] Jonathan Spence, *To Change China: Western advisers in China* (Harmondsworth: Penguin, 1969, 2002 edition), p. 120.

[11] Stanley Wright, *Hart and the Chinese Customs* (Belfast: Mullan and Son, 1950), p. 173.

[12] 5 October 1854, Bruner et al. *Journals, 1854–1863*.

[13] 31 October 1854, Ibid.

[14] Letter to Hughes, dated 9 May 1855, included with a journal entry of 7 May 1855, Ibid. In 1888 we learn that his pony was called St Patrick, after Ireland's patron saint.

[15] Wright, p. 178.

[16] 12 July 1863, Bruner et al. *Journals, 1854–1863*.

[17] Wright, p. 167.

[18] 21 October 1854, Bruner et al. *Journals, 1854–63*.

[19] For a more detailed account of these Irish-born in China see Richard O'Leary, 'Robert Hart in China: The significance of his Irish roots,' *Modern Asian Studies*, 40 (2006) 3.

[20] Letter 544, 1 November 1885. Fairbank et al. *The I.G. in Peking*.

[21] Hart letter to the Association of Ulstermen in London, 22 June 1909, The Robert Hart papers, University of Hong Kong, Box 5.

[22] Wright, p. 859.

[23] Letter 318, 16 February 1881, Fairbank et al. *The I.G. in Peking*.

[24] Letter 121, 13 March 1875, Ibid.

[25] Letter 142, 26 June 1876, Ibid.

4. FROM PATSY O'WANG TO FU MANCHU: IRELAND, CHINA AND RACISM
Fintan O'Toole

[1] 'Eye-Witness Tells of Last Spike Driving,' *Southern Pacific Bulletin*, May 1926 at http://cprr.org/Museum/Farrar/pictures/2005-03-09-02-02.html.

[2] Stanley Aronowitz, *False Promises: The shaping of American working class consciousness* (Durham, NC: Duke University Press, 1992), p. 146.

[3] John Kuo Wei Tchen, *New York before Chinatown: Orientalism and the shaping of American culture* (Baltimore, MD: Johns Hopkins University Press, 2001), p. 217.

[4] Thomas Stewart Denison, 'Patsy O'Wang: An Irish farce with a Chinese mix-up,' in Dave Williams (ed.), *The Chinese Other 1850–1925: An anthology of plays* (Lanham: University Press of America, 1997), pp. 125–48. See also Robert G. Lee, *Orientals: Asian Americans in popular culture* (Philadelphia, PA: Temple University Press, 1999), pp. 78–9.

[5] *The Complete Work of Mark Twain: Sketches new and old* (Alcester, Warks: Read Books, 2008), pp. 277–9.

[6] Edmund Spenser as cited in Seamus Deane (ed.) *The Field Day Anthology of Irish Writing*, Vol. 1. (Derry, Northern Ireland: Field Day Publications, 1991), p. 182.

[7] Fynes Moryson, 'An Itinerary Containing His Ten Yeeres Travell (1617),' *The Field Day Anthology of Irish Writing*, Vol. 1, p. 244.

[8] David Malcolm, *Letters, Essays, and Other Tracts Illustrating the Antiquities of Great Britain and Ireland* (London: J. Millan, 1744), p. 37 ff.

[9] Charles Vallancey, *An Essay on the Antiquity of the Irish Language* (London: Richard Ryan, 1818), p. 57.

[10] James Johnson, *A Tour in Ireland; with meditations and reflections* (London: S. Highley, 1844), pp. 197–8.

[11] Denis Kearney, President, and H. L. Knight, Secretary, 'Appeal from California. The Chinese Invasion. Workingmen's Address,' *Indianapolis Times*, 28 February 1878, at http://www.assumption.edu/users/McClymer/bedford-prototype/toc/KearneyChineseInvasion.html.

[12] Quoted in Krystyn R. Moon, *Yellowface: Creating the Chinese in American popular music and performance* (Piscataway, NJ: Rutgers University Press, 2005), p. 53.

[13] John Kuo Wei Tchen, 'Quimbo Appo's Fear of Fenians: Chinese-Anglo-Irish relations in New York City,' *The New York Irish*, (eds.) Ronald H. Bayor and Timothy J. Meagher (Baltimore, MD: Johns Hopkins University Press, 1996), p. 143.

[14] Samuel Sidney, 'The Australian Colonies and the Gold Supply,' *The Quarterly Review* (London), Vol. 107 January and April 1860, p. 27.

[15] Quoted in John Kuo Wei Chen, 'Quimbo Appo's Fear of Fenians,' *New York Irish*, p. 129.

[16] Ibid., p. 131.

[17] Quoted in Iris Chang, *The Chinese in America: A narrative history* (New York: Viking, 2003), pp. 110–2.

[18] Claudine C. O'Hearn, *Half and Half: Writers on growing up biracial and bicultural* (New York: Pantheon, 1998), p. x.

[19] Ibid., p. 265.

5. Oscar Wilde's Chinese Sage
Jerusha McCormack

[1] *The Speaker*, Vol. 1, No. 6 (February, 1890), reprinted in Richard Ellmann, *The Critic as Artist: The critical writings of Oscar Wilde* (New York: Vintage Books, 1968),

pp. 221–28. All further quotations from this review are from this source. This review appeared thirteen months after the book on which it was based: *Chuang Tsu: Mystic, moralist, and social reformer*, translated by Herbert A. Giles (London, 1889), hereafter cited as *Chuang Tsu* – with quotations given by chapter number.

The translator, Herbert Allen Giles (1845–1935), was then Consul at Tamsui, one of the foremost young sinologists of his day and soon to become the best-known translator of Chinese literature in England. He held the position of Professor of Chinese in Cambridge University from 1897 until 1932.

[2] For a comprehensive list of Wilde's quotations, paraphrases and echoes of Zhuangzi see Isobel Murray, 'Oscar Wilde's Absorption of "Influences": The case history of Chuang Tzu,' *The Durham University Journal*, Vol. 64, no. 1 (December 1971): pp. 1–13. This article is indebted to Murray's pioneering work in identifying borrowings from Zhuangzi by Oscar Wilde.

[3] Of its many chapters, only the first seven are considered as coming authentically from Zhuangzi himself, the 'Outer Chapters' (8–22) and 'Miscellaneous Chapters' (23–33) probably added by disciples over the intervening centuries. This division is credited to the editor, Guo Xiang (Chinese: 郭象; pinyin: Gu Xiàng; Wade-Giles: Kuo Hsiang) d. 312 A.D.

[4] In his review Wilde wrote that, as far as Zhuangzi was concerned, 'true wisdom can neither be learnt nor taught' ('A Chinese Sage,' p. 225). The difference of style is of interest: Wilde works through neatly turned paradox; Zhuangzi simply tells a story.

[5] Mrs Grundy first appeared in Thomas Morton's play called *Speed the Plough* (1798). For an account of her tyranny during the Victorian period, see Walter E. Houghton, *The Victorian Frame of Mind, 1830–1870* (New Haven, CT: Yale University Press, 1957), pp. 397–8. In particular, for a description of the extremes of moral pressure exerted by high Victorian society, see Houghton's chapter on 'Earnestness', pp. 218–262. Such 'earnestness' was of course the target of Wilde's satire in *The Importance of Being Earnest*.

[6] In this context, I refer to the historical Confucius, the writer of the *Analects*. But it is as well to note that 'Confucius' also appears as a fictional character in the writings of Zhuangzi – and that when he does so, he is not only a debating opponent. To the reader's confusion, Zhuangzi often puts his own words into Confucius's mouth: another example of Zhuangzi's rigging of debates.

[7] For Wilde's inversion of Victorian maxims, see Sandra Siegal, 'Wilde's Use and Abuse of Aphorisms,' *Victorian Studies Association of Western Canada* 12 (1986) I, pp. 16–26 and Jerusha McCormack, 'Wilde's Fiction(s),' in Peter Raby (ed.) *The Cambridge Companion to Oscar Wilde* (Cambridge, UK: Cambridge University Press, 1997), pp. 98–9.

[8] In fact, Wilde repudiated the suggestion that his stories were merely for children, saying that in the stories of *The House of Pomegranates* (1891), he had 'about as much intention of pleasing the British child as I had of pleasing the British public'. See Rupert Hart-Davis (ed.) *The Letters of Oscar Wilde* (London: Rupert Hart-Davis, Ltd., 1963), p. 302.

[9] *The Letters of Oscar Wilde*, p. 232. For an extensive exploration of Wilde's sense

of his own Irishness, see Davis Coakley, *Oscar Wilde: The importance of being Irish* (Dublin: Townhouse, 1994).

[10] 'A Chinese Sage,' p. 226. In early 1887, when appointed Chief Secretary for Ireland, Arthur James Balfour (1848–1930) surprised his critics by his ruthless enforcement of the Crimes Act, earning the nickname 'Bloody Balfour'. Balfour's skill for steady administration did much to dispel his reputation as a public lightweight. As a Conservative Member of Parliament, Balfour resisted any overtures to support the Irish Parliamentary Party on Home Rule and, allied with Joseph Chamberlain's Liberal Unionists, strongly encouraged Unionist activism in Ireland.

[11] For a comprehensive, but by no means definitive, study of Wilde's reading, see Thomas Wright, *Oscar's Books* (London: Chatto & Windus, 2008). Ralph Waldo Emerson, for instance, was at this time a key influence. In regard to sources for 'The Soul of Man under Socialism,' see Isobel Murray, 'Oscar Wilde and Individualism: Contexts for *The Soul of Man*,' *Durham University Review* (July 1991), pp. 195-207.

[12] Edouard Roditi is one of two biographers to appreciate the impact of Wilde's reading of Zhuangzi, to which he ascribes the transformation of Wilde from 'an ardent Ruskinian Socialist, with all the naiveté of Romantic idealism' to the sophisticated thinker of *The Soul of Man under Socialism* and *The Critic as Artist*. See *Oscar Wilde* (New York: New Directions, 1986), p. 59, p. 102 and n. 112–113. The other is George Woodcock, who, in *The Double Image of Oscar Wilde* (Montreal: Black Rose Books, 1986), p. 152, notes 'It is clear that the reading of Chuang Tsu's writings had a decisive influence on Wilde's own philosophy, confirming his natural tendencies towards non-action and philosophic anarchism,' adding that Wilde came to agree in many respects with Taoist ideas, 'but … only succeeded in doing so because there was already so much common thought between him and the Chinese sage'. See also pp. 85–8, p. 131, and p.150 f. on commonalities in their thinking.

[13] 'The Soul of Man under Socialism,' *Complete Works of Oscar Wilde*, Merlyn Holland (ed.) (Glasgow: HarperCollins, 1994), p.1182. All further quotations from this essay are from this source.

[14] Murray Rothbard, 'Concepts of the Role of Intellectuals in Social Change Towards Laissez Faire,' *The Journal of Libertarian Studies*, Vol. IX, No.2 (Fall 1990): 43–67 (pp. 45–46). Among other sources may be cited in the work of Ernest Renan, William Morris, that of several Fabians, as well as that of principled anarchists such as Prince Kropotkin.

[15] 'A Chinese Sage,' pp. 221, 222, 226.

[16] 'Soul of Man,' p. 1174.

[17] 'Poems in Prose,' *Complete Works*, pp. 900–1.

[18] W.B. Yeats, quoted in *Oscar Wilde: The critical heritage*, Karl Beckson (ed.) (London: Routledge & Kegan Paul, 1970), p. 398.

[19] 'Soul of Man,' p. 1181. Significantly, perhaps, Wilde did not attribute this quotation directly to Zhuangzi, writing only: 'as a wise man once said many centuries before Christ …'.

[20] 'Soul of Man,' p. 1193.

[21] *Chuang Tsu*, Chapter 30.

[22] 'A Chinese Sage,' p. 223.

[23] 'Soul of Man,' p. 1182.

[24] The first part on 'The True Function and Value of Criticism; with Some Remarks on the Importance of Doing Nothing: A dialogue' was first published in the *Nineteenth Century* for July 1890; the second part appeared in the September issue. Both parts were reprinted, revised and renamed 'The Critic as Artist' in *Intentions* (1891).

[25] *Chuang Tsu*, Chapter 4.

[26] 'The Critic as Artist: Part II,' *Complete Works*, pp. 1121, 1136, 1138–39.

[27] See Charles Baudelaire, 'The Painter of Modern Life: The dandy,' in *Baudelaire: Selected writings on art and artists*, translated by P.E. Charles (Harmondsworth, Middlesex: Penguin, 1972), pp. 419–22.

[28] The formulation is that of Woodcock, *Anarchism*, p. 31. Or, as Prince Paul says in *Vera, or the Nihilists*: 'in good democracy, every man should be an aristocrat'. *Complete Works of Oscar Wilde*, pp. 698–9.

[29] For the role of the dandy in saving people from the dictates of their hearts, see Jerusha McCormack, 'Masks without Faces: The Personalities of Oscar Wilde,' *English Literature in Transition, 1880–1920*, Vol. 22, No. 4 (1979) pp. 253–269.

[30] *Chuang Tsu*, Chapter 2.

[31] 'Wilde and Nietzsche,' in Richard Ellmann (ed.) *Oscar Wilde: A collection of critical essays* (Englewood Cliffs, NJ: Prentice-Hall, 1969), pp. 169–171, citation from p. 169.

[32] W.B. Yeats comments (in 1925) on the popularity of the essay in the Young China party; see Beckson (ed.) *Wilde: The critical heritage*, p. 396. Montgomery Hyde gives the report of Robert Ross in 1908 that copies of the essay, translated into Chinese and Russian, were on sale in the bazaars of Nijni [Nizhny] Novgorod; see Montgomery Hyde, *Oscar Wilde* (London: Eyre Methuen, 1976), p. 381. In regard to Wilde's role in the more comprehensive May Fourth (1919) Movement, see Chow Tse-tsung, *The May Fourth Movement: Intellectual revolution in modern China* (Cambridge, MA: Harvard University Press, 1960), p. 272, p. 273, p. 276.

7. 'Heroism and Zeal': Pioneers of the Irish Christian Missions to China
Patrick Comerford and Richard O'Leary

[1] Letter to Maynooth students, September 1915, Bernard Smyth, *The Chinese Batch: The Maynooth mission to China, origins, 1911–1920* (Dublin: Four Courts, 1994), p. 44.

[2] For histories of the Columban/Maynooth Mission see Smyth, *Chinese Batch*; William Barrett, *The Red Lacquered Gate: The story of Bishop Galvin, co-founder of the Columban Fathers* (New York: Sheed and Ward, 1967); Neil Collins, *The Splendid Cause* (Dublin: Columba Press, forthcoming 2009).

[3] His mother had also thoughtfully redirected to China his gift subscription to the *Cork Examiner*.

[4] Letter to Jim O Connell, 1 November 1913, Smyth, p. 44.

[5] Barrett, p. 75.

[6] Smyth, p. 50.

[7] Barrett, p. 98.

[8] Edmund Hogan, *The Irish Missionary Movement: An historical survey 1830–1980* (Dublin: Gill and Macmillan, 1990), p. 91.

[9] Smyth, p. 74.

[10] Barrett, p. 99.

[11] Smyth, p. 80.

[12] Ibid. p. 84.

[13] Barrett, p. 100.

[14] Michael O'Neill, '1916 and All That,' Columban Central History Archive, Dalgan, code 1916, vol. 1, p. 17.

[15] Hogan, p. 95.

[16] Barrett, p. 118.

[17] Sheila Lucey, *Frances Moloney: Co-founder of the Missionary Sisters of St Columban* (Dublin: Dominican, 1999), p.150.

[18] For a biography of Frances Moloney, see Lucey, 1999.

[19] Lucey, p. 182.

[20] Barrett, p. 155.

[21] See for example Barrett, pp. 273–293.

[22] The story of Dr Sally Wolfe from Skibbereen, a medical missionary in China (1915–1951), is told in her biography by Jane Wright, *She Left Her Heart in China* (Co. Down: Irvine News Agency, 1999).

[23] For histories of the DUFEM, see R.M. Gwynn, E.M. Morton and B.W. Simpson, *TCD in China* (Dublin: Church of Ireland Publishing, 1936, reprinted 1948); and D.M. McFarlan, *Whosoever Plants* (Dublin: DUFEM, 1993).

[24] The other two were William Farmer, who worked briefly in Shanghai, and the Revd Thomas McClatchie, who worked in Shanghai and translated three of the Gospels and parts of the *Book of Common Prayer* into Chinese.

[25] For fuller biographical accounts of these bishops, see Patrick Comerford, *From Mission to Independence: Four Irish bishops in China* (Dublin and Shanghai: DUFEM, 2006) and Jack Hodgins, *Sister Island, History of the Church Missionary Society in Ireland 1814–1994* (Belfast: CMS Ireland, 1997).

[26] Hodgins, pp. 143–4; Comerford, pp. 13–15.

[27] Hodgins, pp. 143–4; Comerford, pp. 14–15.

[28] Comerford, pp. 14–15.

[29] John Hind, *Fukien Memories* (Belfast, 1951).

[30] *The Church Times*, 20 July 1962.

[31] Ibid.

[32] See Max Warren (ed.), *To Apply the Gospel: Selections from the writings of Henry Venn* (Grand Rapids, MI: William B. Eerdmans Publishers, 1971), p. 26, and Roland Allen, *Missionary Methods: Saint Paul's or ours?* (London: World Dominion Press, 2nd edn, 1927), *passim*.

[33] *A History of the Congregations in the Presbyterian Church in Ireland* (Belfast: Presbyterian Historical Society of Ireland, 1982), pp. 342, 447–8, 804.

[34] D.L. Cooney, *The Methodists in Ireland: A short history* (Dublin: The Columba Press, 2001), pp. 244–5; R.L. Cole, *History of Methodism in Ireland* (Belfast: Irish Methodist Publishing, 1960), p. 160; Wright, 1999.

[35] Lu Xiaowen, Richard O'Leary and Yaojun Li, 'Who Are the Believers in Religion in China?' in Abby Day (ed.), *Religion and the Individual* (Aldershot, UK: Ashgate, 2008), pp. 47–64.

[36] DUFEM and the China Educational and Cultural Liaison Committee jointly commissioned the Report by Richard O'Leary and Lan Li, *Mainland Chinese Students and Immigrants in Ireland and their Engagement with Christianity, Churches and Irish Society* (Dublin: DUFEM, 2008).

8. MUSICAL MEETINGS, EAST AND WEST: THE CHIEFTAINS IN CHINA
Hwee-San Tan

[1] See liner notes in *The Chieftains in China*, Dublin: Claddagh Records Ltd, 1984. CC42CD.

[2] For a general introduction to Chinese music, see Alan Thrasher et al. 'China' in S. Sadie and J. Tyrrell (eds) *New Grove Dictionary of Music and Musicians*, 2nd edn.(London: Macmillan, 2001) and J. Lawrence Witzleben et al. 'East Asia: China,' in R. Provine et al. (eds) *Garland Encyclopedia of World Music*, vol. 7 (New York/London: Routledge, 2002).

[3] Annie W. Patterson, 'The Characteristic Traits of Irish Music,' *Proceedings of the Musical Association, 23rd session* (1897), pp. 99–111.

[4] Patterson, p.100.

[5] Patterson, p. 96.

[6] J.A. van Aalst, *Chinese Music*, published by order of the Inspector General of Customs (Shanghai: Statistical Department of the Inspectorate General of Customs, 2nd photolithographical reissue, 1939), p. 36.

[7] Lawrence E. McCullough, 'Style in Traditional Irish Music,' *Ethnomusicology* 21:1 (1977), pp. 85–97.

[8] J. Lawrence Witzleben, '*Silk and Bamboo' Music in Shanghai: the Jiangnan Sizhu instrumental ensemble tradition* (Kent, OH: The Kent State University Press, 1995), p. 89.

[9] *The Chieftains – Full of Joy (Chinese Céilí)*, 1991, YouTube video, http://www.youtube.com/watch?v=38s4mVY2b_Y&feature

[10] John K. Fairbank, Katharine F. Bruner and Elizabeth Matheson (eds), *The I.G. in Peking: Letters of Robert Hart, Chinese Maritime Customs, 1868–1907* (Cambridge, MA: Harvard University Press, 1975) vol. 1, letter no. 395.

[11] This publishing venture probably did not work out, but see Hart's letters to Campbell in letter nos pp. 72, 74, 89, 192. However, among the unpublished materials in the Hart Archive at Queen's University, Belfast, are some loose music manuscript papers with short pieces of untitled music. It is unclear if these are the violin pieces Hart had written.

[12] Fairbank et al. (1975), p. 746.

[13] Juliet Bredon, *Sir Robert Hart: The romance of a great career* (London: Hutchinson & Co., 1909), p. 186.

[14] A brass band first appeared in the film *Malu Tianshi* ('The Angel of the Roads') in 1937; in 1931, a brass band was used in the funeral of the Shanghai Baghdad-born tycoon Silas Aaron Hardoon. See Francesca Tarocco, *The Cultural Practices of Modern Chinese Buddhism: Attuning the dharma* (London and New York: Routledge, 2007), p. 109.

[15] Fairbank et al. (1975), p. 1281.

[16] Ibid., p. 774.

[17] Ibid., p. 458.

[18] Ibid., p. 464.

[19] Robert Ronald Campbell, *James Duncan Campbell, a Memoir by his Son* (Cambridge, MA: East Asian Research Center, Harvard University, 1970), p. 55.

[20] Jonathan Spence, *Emperor of China: Self-portrait of K'ang-hsi* (London: Jonathan Cape Ltd, 1974), p. 73.

[21] J. J. Amiot et al., *De la musique des chinois tant anciens que modernes* (Paris: chez Nyon, 1780). Some of Amiot's own compositions can be heard on Joseph-Marie Amiot, *Messe des jesuites de pekin*, Auvidis France, 1998, E 8642.

[22] Jean-Baptiste Du Halde, *Description géographique, historique, chronologique, politique et physique de l'Empire de la Chine*, English trans. by Richard Brookes, 2 vols (London: printed by T. Gardner for Edward Cave, 1738–41).

[23] van Aalst, p. 12.

[24] Campbell, p. 55.

[25] Wang Zhaoyu 1958, p. 23, as cited in Han Kuo-huang and Judith Gray, 'The Modern Chinese Orchestra,' *Asian Music* 11(1): p. 18.

[26] See Martin Stokes, 'Place, Exchange and Meaning: Black Sea musicians in the West of Ireland,' in M. Stokes (ed.), *Ethnicity, Identity and Music: The musical construction of place* (Oxford: Berg, 1994), pp. 97–115.

[27] This was the 12th International CHIME (European Foundation for Chinese Music Research) Conference, of which I was convener.

10. Urban Planning in China: Mega-cities and Beyond
Pauline Byrne

[1] http://www.epsiplus.net/content/pdf/1849

[2] 'China's urbanization encounters "urban disease"' on www.chinanews.cn (18 November 2005).

[3] Prof. Dr Wu Jiang, Shanghai Urban Planning Bureau, *Shanghai Master Plan 1999–2020*.

[4] 'Losing Heart and Soul?' *Urban Land,* May 2007, p. 24.

[5] Bosbach, Roland, Wood & Zapata Architects, Architects for Xintiandi, Shanghai.

[6] Clifford, Coonan, 'Getting Jiggy at the Great Ball of China,' *Irish Times,* 20 August 2007.

[7] 'In Brief,' *Planning,* 7 December 2007, p. 3.

[8] 2006 estimate on http://www.china-embassy.org/eng/gyzg/t364350.htm

[9] 'Open Document International Federation of Red Cross and Red Crescent Societies' on http://www.reliefweb.int/rw/RWB.NSF/db900SID/HMYT-6S9QGP?

[10] 'Big Increase in EU Car Ownership,' *Sunday Business Post*, 15 October 2006.

[11] 'China Leads Way of Reducing Ppoverty,' report on www.chinadaily.com.cn/china (9 October 2007).

[12] Rachel Levitt, 'Lost in Discussion: Weak market city potential,' *Urban Land*, May 2007, p. 16.

11. CHINA COMES TO IRELAND
Ruadhán Mac Cormaic

[1] Frank N. Pieke, 'Introduction' in Benton and Pieke (eds), *The Chinese in Europe* (London: Palgrave Macmillan, 1998), p. 1.

[2] Ibid.

[3] Xiang Biao, 'Emigration from China: A sending country perspective' in *International Migration*, vol. 41 (3), September 2003, p. 27.

[4] Of those who identified themselves as Chinese in the 2006 census, over 70 per cent were single, 40 per cent were aged between 15 and 24 while another 50 per cent were in the 25–44 bracket. Census 2006, Central Statistics Office, www.cso.ie.

[5] Dr Lan Li and Dr Richard O'Leary, 'Mainland Chinese Students and Immigrants in Ireland, and their Engagement with Christianity, Churches and Irish Society' (Dublin University Far Eastern Mission, March 2008).

[6] Nicola Yau, 'Celtic Tiger, Hidden Dragon: Exploring identity among second generation Chinese in Ireland,' *Translocations: Migration and social change*, vol. 2, issue 1, Summer 2007, www.translocations.ie.

[7] Alice Feldman, Mary Gilmartin, Steven Loyal and Bettina Migge, 'Getting On – From Migration to Integration: Chinese, Indian and Lithuanian and Nigerian migrants' experiences in Ireland,' published by the Immigrant Council of Ireland, May 2008, p. 80. The report found that just 1 per cent of Chinese respondents said they were politically active, while the same percentage told researchers they were involved in trade unions. The figures for other groups were higher: 7 per cent of Indians, 8 per cent of Lithuanians and 25 per cent of Nigerians were involved in unions.

[8] Li and o'Leary, p. 50.

[9] Ibid. p. 13.

[10] Feldman et al. p. 127.

[11] Ying Yun Wang with Dr Rebecca King-O'Riain, 'Chinese Students in Ireland,' Community Profiles Series (Dublin: National Consultative Committee on Racism and Interculturalism, September 2006), p. 36.

[12] Feldman et al. pp. 155–6

[13] Interview with the author, November 2007.

[14] Feldman et al., p. 105.

[15] Li and O'Leary, p. 47.

[16] Interview with the author, November 2007.

[17] Language student quoted in Wang, p. 46.

[18] Language student quoted in Li and O'Leary, p. 49.

[19] Interview with the author, November 2007.

[20] Despite the encouragement of the Chinese government, a majority of Chinese students do not return home on completion of their studies overseas. In the United States, the return rate of Chinese students over the period 1978–99 was only 14.1 per cent, while just one-third of Chinese students in Japan are reported to return home. Nearly half the Chinese students in Europe return home – in France the return rate from 1978–99 was 47.6 per cent and in the United Kingdom 46.8 per cent. Frank Laczko, 'Understanding Migration between China and Europe' in *International Migration*, vol. 41 (3), September 2003, p. 9.

[21] Interview with the author, November 2007.

[22] Quoted in Li and O'Leary, p. 51.

[23] Quoted in Nicola Yau, p. 3.

[24] Robin Cohen, foreword to Chan Kwok-bun, *Migration, Ethnic Relations and Chinese Business* (London: Routledge, 2005).

Index

INDEX